A PREFACE TO
THE MAGIC FLUTE

Dress designs and play-bill for a performance of *The Magic Flute*, Leipzig, c. 1820.

THE STUDENT'S MUSIC LIBRARY—HISTORICAL AND CRITICAL SERIES

Edited by PERCY M. YOUNG

A PREFACE TO THE MAGIC FLUTE

by

E. M. BATLEY
B.A., M.Litt.

Senior Lecturer in German, Goldsmiths' College

London
DENNIS DOBSON

TO
MY WIFE

First published in Great Britain in 1969 by
Dobson Books Ltd., 80 Kensington Church Street, London, W.8
Printed by Clarke, Doble & Brendon Ltd.,
Plymouth

SBN 234 77205 0

CONTENTS

		Page
List of Illustrations		7
Foreword		9
Author's Note		11
List of Abbreviations		12
1.	Old Viennese Popular Theatre	13
2.	The Conflict between Old Viennese Popular Theatre and Literary Drama in the Kärntnerthortheater	27
3.	Philipp Hafner and the Growth of Popular Viennese Traditions	37
4.	The Growth of Singspiel in Southern Germany	61
5.	Emanuel Schikaneder and the Viennese Singspiel after 1789	77
6.	Schikaneder's Viennese Singspiele prior to The Magic Flute	93
7.	The Magic Flute and its disputed Authorship	105
8.	The Unity of Schikaneder's Libretto	114
Notes		131
Bibliography		165
Index		171

LIST OF ILLUSTRATIONS

frontispiece

Dress designs and play-bill for a performance of *The Magic Flute*, Leipzig, *c.* 1820

facing page

Page of the MS score in Mozart's hand   48

The Queen of Night's entry, Act II, Munich, 1818; by Simon Quaglio   49

Tamino, design by Joseph Hoffmann   64

Sarastro, design by Joseph Hoffman   65

Papageno, by Ignaz Alberti, from the first programme-book   96

"Here by beauties, I give you my birds", Act I; by Geyl and Nessthaler, Brünn, 1794   97

Finale, Act I; première in Schikaneder's Freihaustheater, 1791; by Geyl and Nessthaler   112

Emanuel Schikaneder, by Philipp Richter   113

With the exception of plates II, VI and IX these illustrations are reproduced by kind permission of the photo archives of the Austrian National Library, Vienna.

FOREWORD

It is hoped that in some way this book can help to restore a balance of historical perspective which since 1791 has been gradually upset in favour of an all too one-sided appraisal of the textual qualities of *The Magic Flute*. For these reasons the author has seen fit to give some account of the Old Viennese Popular Theatre and its representatives many years prior to the first appearance of the opera in 1791. He shares the view that the work is not merely the creation of a musical genius, but also the contribution of a playwright whose experience as an actor-manager was deeply and inextricably rooted in popular traditions which were being established much earlier at the beginning of the century.

No one in the twentieth century would wish to dispute the immortal qualities given to the opera by Mozart's music, but in the eighteenth century a musician was frequently "snubbed" and found his name either merely appended at the end of the *Singspiel*, as in the case of Joseph Haydn's *Der neue krumme Teufel*, or billed in small print as on the occasion of the première of *The Magic Flute*. Neither Haydn nor Mozart took offence although critics since then have unwisely elected to do so.

At that time in Southern Germany the librettist and his libretto were the moving forces behind the production of musical works for the stage, as is further born out, for instance, by the large quantities of unaccompanied dialogue in the *Singspiel*. As a result of the still dominant influence of the Baroque age in Vienna the visual rather than the musical aspect was regarded, certainly by the audience, as the more important. It is from this viewpoint that the author has chosen to treat the theatrical environment of *The Magic Flute*.

It is clear that such treatment may be representative, but it is certainly not exhaustive. Little mention has been made, for instance, of the priesthood in the opera. A discussion on whether or not the priesthood was specifically intended to portray a masonic brotherhood, an issue which as yet the author sees as by

9

no means satisfactorily resolved, would be of some interest, but would not make any further significant contribution to the particular theatrical picture the book seeks to convey.

Wherever possible, reference has been made to original texts but the author would like to express his gratitude to the writers of two invaluable secondary sources: Professor O. Rommel and his book *Die Alt-Wiener Volkskomödie* and Professor E. Komorzynski's biography of Emanuel Schikaneder. Some of the material in three chapters of the book has been published previously by the author. Most of the chapter on *Singspiel* in Southern Germany first appeared as an article in *German Life and Letters* (April, 1966) and earlier versions of the last two chapters in *Music and Letters* (July, 1965) and *The Music Review* (May, 1966) respectively. The author thanks the editors of these journals for their kind permission to print in book form.

He would like also to express his thanks to the music, theatre and photo archives of the Viennese Austrian National Library, the Viennese City Library, the Mozart museum in Salzburg, the British Museum and the facilities offered by its Reading Room, and the University Libraries of Durham, Newcastle and Leeds. A personal debt of gratitude is owed to Professor Komorzynski and to the late Professor O. E. Deutsch for the ready interest they expressed in the work undertaken and to Professor D. F. S. Scott, Professor of German at Durham University, for his constant encouragement.

AUTHOR'S NOTE

Many of the extracts quoted in this book were printed originally at a time when the present method of vowel mutation in New High German had not been standardized. In view of the typographical difficulties of reproducing its earlier rendering, the modern form has been adopted throughout. Archaisms and irregularities in spelling, inflection, punctuation and grammar generally, have been amended at the author's discretion in cases where the meaning tended to become obscure.

The translations provided in the Notes are intended to help those readers having no knowledge of German to a quick understanding of the passages quoted. In those cases where a particular point, style or rhyme scheme has seemed to the author to be of paramount importance, he has attempted to reproduce the same in the translation.

LIST OF ABBREVIATIONS

Bd. (vol.)   Band (volume).

Jhrg.   Jahrgang (year).

LM   Leopold Mozart.

M. Bt 1.   *Die Maschinenkomödie* Barocktradition 1. ed. O. Rommel (Leipzig, 1935).

MM   Marie Anne Thekla Mozart.

MmeM   Madame Mozart.

mus.   music.

SW.   Sämtliche Werke (collected works).

WHTA   Wiener Hoftheateralmanach 1804.

WM   Wolfgang Amadeus Mozart.

OLD VIENNESE POPULAR THEATRE

In the early half of the eighteenth century German drama was by no means as advanced or refined as that of England and France. It is true to say that, as a form of literary art, it hardly existed at all and could achieve only crude and popular representation on the strolling stage. Where theatre was established in the country, as in the private residences of the rulers of the various principalities which then comprised Germany, it mostly relied on literary offerings from abroad. The country as a whole remained oblivious to its lack of a national drama. The strolling stage of Germany, however, did much to compensate for this. Although it could offer very little of literary worth, it appealed to that class of people to which the court theatre did not, and in so doing turned popular, unrefined, but native material to that end. Initially, there was of course some considerable influence from abroad, but this steadily diminished as a theatre arose which had its own individual character.

By its very nature the strolling stage was more concerned with entertaining than with uplifting its audience, and its repertoire naturally favoured comedy. From the end of the sixteenth century the popular continental stage had been greatly affected by the style of theatre offered by the *Englische Comödianten*. These players travelled extensively throughout Europe, adapting their repertoire—which included seven dramas of Shakespeare[1]—to the demands of the strolling stage. In their ranks appeared the popular comedian whose allotted task it was to amuse the audience with his comic antics and joke-ridden commentary on the action of the play. He became known under a variety of names, each representing a national dish: Jak Pudding (England), Stockfisch or Pickelhering (Netherlands), Jean Potage (France), Signor Macaroni (Italy) and Hans Wurst (Germany). The presence on stage of the so-called *Lustigmacher* (*Merry-Maker*), where all else remained subordinate to his comedy, was an obstacle to any aesthetic development of the genre. The organic demands of characterization and the planned climax of a literary play remained irrelevant issues. The only move in the right direction, and even this was slight, came as the variety of nomenclature disappeared and the popular comedian became known simply as Pickelhering.[2]

At the beginning of the eighteenth century the influence of the *commedia dell' arte* began to make itself felt on the popular stage in Germany, at first, however, in the shape of only one of its original figures—Harlequin. On the Viennese stage it was not until the 1730's that other characters from the *commedia* began to proliferate. Harlequin's influence appears, moreover, to have been restricted to one of name alone. He assumed, more or less, the rôle of the Pickelhering of the earlier *Englische Comödianten*, and was often mistaken for him. Herzog Ernst August of Hannover referred to him as "now Pickelhering, now Harlequin" and in the prologue to *Les comédiens esclaves*, which was performed in Vienna's *Nouveau Théâtre Italien* in 1726, Harlequin revealed how closely his function resembled Pickelhering's.

> Mein Geschäft ist, mich wohl oder übel der Aufträge zu entledigen, die man mir gibt, bald dumm, bald geistreich zu sein, Stockschläge zu geben oder zu empfangen, die einen zu täuschen, den andern einen Gefallen zu tun, verliebt zu sein, gefrässig (Gourmand), Faulenzer, Trunkenbold.[3]

Joseph Anton Stranitzky (1676-1727),[4] the founder of the Old Viennese Popular Theatre, was playing in the city's New Market in 1706: in 1708 he opened a theatre in the dance-hall in Teinfalt Street and in 1712 replaced the Italian company in the Kärntnerthortheater, paying 2,000 Fl. per annum to lease the theatre, and an additional 1,300 Fl. tax for the poor.[5] This provided the popular plays of the strolling stage with their first residential theatre. Stranitzky has also been acknowledged as the creator of the original Viennese Hans Wurst, a popular comedian most probably derived from Pickelhering, with whose character Stranitzky must have come into contact before he came to Vienna, when he was a member of Magister Velthen's strolling company. It is known that the latter often included Pickelhering's extempore comedy in his repertoire.[6] Under Stranitzky the popular comedian became more distinctive in appearance: he

14

wore a prescribed costume and accoutrements, he let it be known that he originated from Salzburg, and he acknowledged himself as of the peasant class. Smekal gives an account of his appearance:

Hans Wurst trat auf mit einem hohen grünen Spitzhut, das Haar in einem stehenden Zipfel hinaufgebunden, die dick und scharf bezeichneten Augenbrauen bis zur Nase zusammengezogen. Er trug einen spitzen Vollbart und einen kleinen Schnurrbart ohne Fliege über dem Mund, der damit ausdrucksvoll frei blieb, eine grosse weisse Krause um den Hals. Eine Joppe mit langen, engen Ärmeln liess den grünen Brustfleck sehen, auf dem ein grosses Herz mit aufgenähten Buchstaben H W figurierte, die Hosen waren lang und unten zugebunden, am Rücken hing das dicke, wurstförmige Ränzel, das ihm den Namen gegeben, an der Seite die hölzerne Pritsche, die Füsse steckten in Bundschuhen. Am meisten bezeichnend mag wohl der Brustfleck erschienen sein, dessen auch die Stücke wiederholt Erwähnung tun. Gefragt, ob er ein Herz habe, erwiderte Hans Wurst: "Ja, auf dem Brustfleck."[7]

So clearly defined did Hans Wurst become, that Stranitzky's successor made no essential deviation from the original. The group improvisation practised by the *commedia dell' arte* did not influence the form of the Viennese popular plays until after 1727, the year of Stranitzky's death, and until that time he remained the most prominent individual and comedian of the theatre. He was not, however, impregnable against other influences from Italy and he adapted the lavish décor of the baroque theatre of the Viennese Imperial Court to provide Hans Wurst with an elevated backcloth for his farcical peregrinations, the bathos of the spectacle exaggerating the comedy. The following, incongruous assembly illustrates his style:

Der Tiber-Fluss, auf der Seiten hervor ein schöner Kunstgartten mit schattigen Bäumen, Julius Antonius, Lucius Scipio und HW. auf den Gondeln. (Cicero, II, 8).[8]

The artificiality of musical composition in the Italian style, the pure showmanship of coloratura singing, and the cosmopolitan libretti, did not appear on Stranitzky's stage. His 14 *Haupt- und Staatsaktionen*, dated 1724,[9] would appear to minimize the importance of music in his theatre. For the most part these were adaptations of libretti from the *opera seria* of the Viennese

15

Imperial Court and it is perhaps indicative of Stranitzky's attitude to music that the arias from the original operas were either not reproduced at all in the *Haupt- und Staatsaktionen* or they were translated into German prose. As in Shakespeare, those parts of the dialogue to which the writer wished to draw attention—for example, the closing lines of scenes and acts—were written in rhymed verse. That Stranitzky did not transfer the music of Italian opera to his own stage, can in no way be regarded as an indication that his theatre had no musical interest, for indeed it had; but it does show that music occupied a position subservient to comedy.[10]

From 1712 to 1727, the duration of Stranitzky's activity in the Play House in the Square by the Carinthian Gate, his theatre remained a popular one. It did, however, show signs of development, for the characters who appeared on Stranitzky's stage had advanced beyond the psychologically static and unreal figures of Jesuit drama, which had been content to give representation to moral ideas and allegory. Stranitzky's allegiance was not to the church, nor to a consideration of eternal life, but to everyday, worldly events. The external trappings of baroque drama, the ghosts, spirits, magicians, devils and allegories, virtually disappear, and where Stranitzky does make use of them, their associations are clearly popular and secular:

> Wie der Teuffel diese Beschwörung gehöret, und dass er ihm sein böses Weib wolle herbringen, so ist der Teuffel also erschrocken, dass er durch Himmel und Hölle um Pardon gebetten, ist auch auf der Stell nicht allein gehorsamlich ausgefahren, sondern hat auch alle sein vornhin gewonnenes Geld dem Kräuter-Männle, wenn er nur sein böses Weib nicht kommen lasse, freywillig verehret. Seht Herr! auch so gar der Teuffel förchtet sich vor einem bösen Weib.[11]

Refinement is unknown and the theatre remains free of the inhibitions of aristocratic entertainment:

> Ich habe zwar ein wenig ein dicken Hintern, aber mein Doctor hat mir versprochen, dass er mir solchen vertreiben wolle, und zwar mit einer Ziegen-Molcken... Er versichert mich, dass es nur gewisse humors acres sind, welche sich durch das Diaphragma und Mensenterium ausbreiten, und endlich hinunter in das Sitzbret fallen.[12]

16

The course of Stranitzky's plots is still determined by frequent misunderstandings and the miscarriage of letters, but the human element grows in importance, and disguises disappear almost completely. The theme of love—a necessary adjunct of the real and popular world—attains a degree of status, although like all other facets of the popular theatre in its early days, it has to remain subservient to the demands of comedy. A full stomach is preferred to a love-sick heart, sentimentality is decried as an unhealthy folly:

HERRN: Warum soll ich nicht so verliebt seyn als du?

FUCHSMUNDI: Als ich? Ja wann ihr es machet wie ich, so würdet ihr nicht so mager werden und vor Ungedult verschmachten. Wenn ich gleich noch so verliebt bin, so thue ich mir gleichwohl auch was zu gute. Wenn ich ein glass Wein von einer frischen lebhaften Farbe vor mir habe, nebst einem wohlproportionirten Capaun der eine schöne erhabene Brust hat, so vergisse ich alsbald alle andere Lapperey und denke weder an Isabellen noch Rosalien noch an alles solches Geschmeiss, die einem alles im Leibe verwirret machen.

HERRN: Wirst du bald fertig seyn?

FUCHSMUNDI: Das ist erst der Eingang meiner Rede, ich bin noch lange nicht an dem Text. . .[13]

Fuchsmundi, who was to be known from 1712 as the Hans Wurst, continues to advise his master in the affairs of the heart and, in so doing, voices what is to become one of the traditional aspects of the popular theatre, the decrying of the married state:

FUCHSMUNDI: Mein Herr! Ihr sollet diese Heurrath bleiben lassen, wann ihr nicht in die grosse Welt-Bruderschafft der Fratrum Corneliorum kommen wollet, allwo ihr zwar gekronet, aber von andern ausgelacht werden sollet und ist bey dieser Zeit gar nichts neues um solche grosse Hirschen, die sich auf dem Plan dieser Welt sehen lassen, und ist die Liebe bey der Zeit gantz gefährlich, dass solche wohl mit jenem sprechen können:
  Ihr Leute gebt mirs doch geschrieben,
  Dass ich ein Erz-Phantaste bin,
  Und sollte mir es nicht belieben,
  So bringt mich mit Gewalt dahin,
  Dass ich die Thorheit, zum Beschluss,
  Vor aller Welt bekennen muss.
  Ich höre nichts mit meinen Ohren,
  Ich bin mit sehenden Augen blind,

Der Mund hat allen Schmack verlohren,
Die Fäuste sind nicht, wer sie sind,
Die Nase reucht, und hat gleichwohl
Den Schnuppen, wann sie riechen soll.
Dem Schedel fehlt ein grosser Sparren,
Das Haupt ist wie ein Tauben-Haus,
Da fliegen mir die jungen Narren,
Bald vornen ein, bald hinten raus,
Doch auf den Abend ziehn sie hier
Zusammen wieder ins Quartier.
Wollt ihr kein bleussgen bauen lassen,
Darein ich mich versperren kan,
So hetzt die Kinder auf der Strassen,
Mit Hund und Katzen auf mich an,
Und legt mir alle Namen zu,
Biss icht nicht mehr so närrisch thu.
Verbrennt mir nur den Kopff mit Schellen,
Und setzt mir einen Fuchsschwanz auf,
Wollt ihr mir einen Hut bestellen,
So flickt mir auch ein Kuhhorn drauf,
Und gebt mir an des Säbels statt,
Ein Holz, das keine Scheide hat.
Besetzt mein Kleid mit bunten Flecken,
Und macht mirs Band von Bohnenstroh,
Und schreibt mir an auf allen Ecken,
Diss ist ein Narr in Folio.
Wofern ich bey dem Narren-Spiel,
Nicht zum Erkänntnis kommen will.[14]

A later sketch in the *Ollapatrida*, entitled "A certain Officer
advises Fuchsmundi to become a Captain in the War/then he
will certainly win Miss Teresel for his bride",[15] where the comedy
arises from the contrast between the unusually conscientious
heroism of the officer and the not so heroic but more practical
Fuchsmundi, also contains elements which were to become embodied in the tradition of the Viennese Popular Theatre. Thus
the justifiable timorousness of Fuchsmundi in this scene recurred
later in 1791 in Papageno, the popular comedian in *The Magic
Flute*. The public's general interest, also in the theatrical presentation of aspects of military life, further stimulated by Joseph
II's aggrandisement of Austria's army, led to the development in
the 1770's and 80's of a military genre, the "Soldatenstück", or
"Ritterdrama". On the one hand this was to be readily adopted

18

by the playwrights of the *Sturm und Drang* and to find some degree of expression in Goethe's *Götz von Berlichingen* (1773) and Schiller's *Die Räuber* (1781); on the other it was to influence the impresario of the strolling stage, Emanuel Schikaneder, who later incorporated the military spectacle in his productions for the Viennese suburban theatres. A relationship with the *miles gloriosus* of the *commedia dell' arte* may also be surmised.

Shortly before his death in 1727, Stranitzky was said to have introduced his successor, Gottfried Prehauser (1699-1769), to the audience of the Kärntnerthortheater. Prehauser, too, had had experience of the strolling stage. He was ably equipped to continue the tradition of the comedy established by the creation of the first Viennese Hans Wurst, but the management of the theatre had to be transferred to two Italians. These were Borosini, a Court singer, and Selliers, a Court dancer and writer of ballet. On the occasion of Prehauser's first entry on to the stage of the theatre, Stranitzky, who was in ill health, spoke of his approaching death and asked for permission to recommend his successor to the audience. An oppressive silence met his words as he brought on Prehauser from the wings, but the latter took advantage of the situation, fell on his knees, arms outstretched to the audience, and in a droll voice made his appeal: "Bitte, lachen Sie über mich!" ("Please laugh at me!") This the audience did, and Prehauser's future success was assured.[16]

In the main Prehauser persisted with the traditional costume of the Hans Wurst, but the essential character of the popular comedian inevitably altered under the influence of a new personality. He was a more volatile wit than Stranitzky had been and his flexibility allowed him to be more easily associated with the city life of Vienna. The grotesque bathos of the *Haupt- und Staatsaktion* was no longer the order of the day. Prehauser was accorded some honour even in literary drama. Smekal refers to Prehauser's "genius as an actor" and the *Wiener Hoftheater-almanach* of 1804 reports his success in the role of Just in Lessing's *Minna von Barnhelm*, where "not for one moment was one reminded of Hans Wurst".[17] Both as actor and as comedian Prehauser has been described as having greater talents than his predecessor, and on this point no dissentient voice has been noted. Gradually he attracted around him in the Kärntner-thortheater a team of predominantly extempore comedians and improvisation was transformed from instances of spontaneous outbursts to what might be called improvisation in the round. In the first volume of the collected works of Philipp Hafner,[18] a talented improvisator and comedian, who wrote plays for Prehauser's *Stegreifensemble*, the editor, Joseph Sonnleithner, has included the sketch of an extempore play, prepared by Mayberg, a member of the company, in 1749.[19] Sonnleithner's declared intention is to show thereby the style of the popular theatre at that time. The title alone *Der steinreiche aber sackgrobe Bernardon. Colombina, die zanksüchtige und alles widersprechende Land-Dame. Hans Wurst, der muntere Gärtner bey einer stets zanken-den Frau.* ('The filthy-rich but crude and coarse Bernardon. Colombina, the argumentative and completely contradictory country lady. Hans Wurst, the jolly gardener in the service of a woman who natters constantly'.), as also the scenes which Sonnleithner has chosen to include, illustrate the wider interplay of Prehauser's comedy, and Sonnleithner's words in the preface underline further the importance of improvisation in the round :

> Den extemporirten Stücken lag immer ein Canevas zum Grunde, der desto magrer seyn durfte, da die spielenden Personen genau wussten, worinn die komische Kraft jeder einzelnen vorzüglich bestand, und da sie vollkommen zusammen gewohnt waren; die einzige Bedingung, unter welcher das sogenannte Ensemble, eine ganz, wenn ich so sagen darf, runde Vorstellung erreichbar ist.[20]

No longer was the form of the Viennese popular play determined by the *lazzi* of one comedian, but instead by group improvisation in the manner of the earlier *commedia dell' arte*. New prominence was given to the supporting cast, and Hans Wurst, although still occupying the position of first comedian, was not so much the focal point of comic interest that he could continue to upset the balance in the form of the popular play. Several minor comedians emerged during this period to enrich the heritage of the Old Viennese Popular Theatre.

Prehauser's *Stegreifensemble* consisted of a variety of German and Italian actors and actresses. In 1727, the year of Stranitzky's death, Andreas Schröter and Anna Maria Nuth registered at the theatre, and later the latter's husband—Franz Anton—was to provide the company with several scenes from the *commedia dell' arte*. In 1728 Signor Canzacchi came to the theatre from the

Italian company. Friedrich Wilhelm Weiskern was engaged in 1734 and he provided countless burlesques based on Italian, Spanish and French models. Johann Mayberg joined the company in 1743, Joseph Huber in 1745 and Anton Brenner in 1755. Other members were J. E. Leinhaas, who had registered in 1727, and Johann Christoph Gottlieb. The extremely successful comedian, Joseph Kurz, registered in 1737 and was joined by his wife in 1744. As a mark of the temporary success of the ensemble, Gottlob Heydrich and Christiane Friedrike Lorenzin, who had originally enlisted in the service of literary drama as it struggled to find its feet in the same theatre, chose to join the exponents of extempore acting. The attempt to establish literary drama in the same building unwittingly provided the ensemble with material for its burlesque, much in the same way as Italian *opera seria* and the baroque theatre had served Stranitzky as a backcloth for his brand of comedy. It was not uncommon, for instance, for Lessing's dramas to appear embellished with "Hans Wurst follies".

The summary history of the Old Viennese Popular Theatre in the theatre almanac of 1804 describes the spirit of the ensemble at this time as competitive, and in this atmosphere each member created and developed his own popular figure. Names of some of the stock characters of the *commedia dell' arte* inevitably appeared in this respect: Harlequin was played by Franz Anton Nuth, but still as a minor comedian, corresponding to his original rôle in the *commedia*, and his wife won local fame as Colombina, the soubrette who came to be accepted as Hans Wurst's female counterpart. Schröter played the parts of Bramarbas and Capitino, the *miles gloriosus* of the *commedia*, and Leinhaas introduced Pantalon to the Viennese stage. The paternal tyrant, Odoardo, was portrayed by Weiskern, and Truffaldino by Canzacchi. Less important names from the point of view of comedy, but nevertheless quite frequent ones, were Dottore, Scapin, Pierrot, Rosaura, Lelio, Anselmo, Leander, Angelika, Angela, Rosamunda and Rosalia. Scaramouche, Mezzetin, Brighella, Francatrippa and Tartaglia did not appear in the Viennese popular theatre.

There also emerged at this time a number of minor comic figures of German conception. Anton Brenner's Burlin was one of these, although he may have derived from the popular Don

Juan. In Hafner's play *Etwas zum Lachen im Fasching* ("Something to laugh at in Fasching") Burlin even attained the rank of first comedian. The play was also performed on the strolling stage. Joseph Huber created the popular comedian Leopoldl, thus providing the famous character-comedian of the later Leopoldstadttheater, Anton Hasenhut, with a model for his own creation, Thaddädl, the latter appearing as a companion figure to Johann Laroche's Kasperl. Gottlieb provided the theatre with Jackerl, a comedian of distinctly peasant origins, and the comedian who enjoyed the greatest success, being subordinate in his comic function only to Hans Wurst, was a man of noble descent, Joseph Kurz, whose creation was known by the name of Bernardon, "a young, insolent and slovenly lout."[21]

By this time magic and music had been incorporated in the productions of the theatre in an attempt to attract a large audience within its doors. The *Teutsche Arien*, a collection of comic songs, which had been compiled with this purpose in mind and which were in the repertoire from 1737 until 1757, revealed that the policy of the present theatre was the same as that which had governed Stranitzky's theatre. Just as the latter had mocked the elevated tone of *opera seria* by placing his Salzburg peasant alongside the metaphysical symbols of Italian heroics, so did the arias now parody the effusive love-declaration of *opera seria* in the popularized language of Hans Wurst and Colombina:

HANS WURST:
Columbine, kleine Maus!
Schöner als ein Veigerlstrauss!

COLUMBINE:
Wurstl, allerliebstes Herz,
Weicher als Spinat und Stertz!

HANS WURST:
Weisser als wie Kreid und Schnee!

COLUMBINE:
Milder als ein Kräuteltee![22]

Kurz parodied the same Italian characters of rank and the melodramatic, baroque consciousness of the fleeting passage of time:

O du arme Welt!
Du nimmst ja nicht in acht

Dass jeder Augenblick das Leben kürzer macht.
O du arme Welt!
So bist du jetzt bestellt,
Auf Wortl, und auf Lügen,
Den Nächsten zu betrügen,
Sein Glücke zu beneiden,
Die Ehre abzuschneiden,
  Bald singen,
  Bald springen,
Bald sauffen, bald ranzen,
Bald spielen, bald tanzen,
  Bald Steyrisch,
  Bald Schwäbisch,
  Hanackisch,
  Slavakisch,
Bald walzen umatum,
He sa rum rum,
  O du arme Welt,
  Wie bist du jetzt bestellt.[23]

(Der aufs neue begeisterte und belebte Bernardon)

The main features of Italian opera are presented to the audience of the popular theatre as things beyond human understanding. In the following extract from the same source as the above, Isabella is the female epitome of Italian opera and, in providing the foil to the melodrama, Hans Wurst shows the same lack of appreciation as would the audience of the Kärntnerthortheater:

ISABELLA:
  Ich fühle in der Brust ein rechtes Höllenfeuer,
  Ich börste fast vor Zorn, vor Rache und vor Wut, (*zu Hans Wurst*).
  Komm her, verschlinge mich grausames Ungeheuer.

HANS WURST (*forchtsam*):
  Ach wär ich dasmal fort, das wär für mich recht gut.
  Madame, ich bin der Bräutigam.

ISABELLA (*freundlich*):
  Ja, ja, ich kenne dich,
  Du bist, der mein Herz nahm (*sie umarmen sich*).
  Ach! komme.

HANS WURST:
  Da bin ich.

ISABELLA (*rasend, stösst Hans Wurst von sich*):
Fort Basilisque, fort Crocotil,
Nach Blut geht nur dein Durst.

HANS WURST:
Bey meiner Treu, das ist zu viel,
Ich bin ja der Hans Wurst.

ISABELLA (*freundlich*):
Mein Engel, komm, umarme mich.

HANS WURST (*forchtsam, umarmet sie*):
Was wird wol noch daraus.

ISABELLA (*mit Dolch*):
Stirb Mörder, Schelm hab ich dich.

HANS WURST (*ängstig*):
O Weh! Jetzt ist es aus.

ISABELLA:
Wilst du lieben?

HANS WURST:
Ja.

ISABELLA:
Wilst du sterben?

HANS WURST:
Na.

ISABELLA:
Wilst du lieben?

HANS WURST:
Ja.

ISABELLA:
Wilst du sterben?

HANS WURST:
Na.

ISABELLA:
Wilst du sterben?

HANS WURST:
Na.

ISABELLA:
Wilst du lieben?

HANS WURST:
Ja.

ISABELLA:
Wilst du lieben?

HANS WURST:
    Ja.
ISABELLA:
    Wilst du sterben?

HANS WURST:
    Na.
ISABELLA:
    Nun wolan, so solst du lieben.

HANS WURST:
    Wär ich doch zu Haus geblieben.

ISABELLA (*serieus*):
    Höre meinen Entschluss an:
    Du solst mit mir stets in Plagen,
    Ja in Jammer, Angst, und Noht
    Deine Lebenszeit zutragen,
    Endlich folgt darauf der Tod.
    Unsre Eh, sey Qual und Weh.

HANS WURST (*adagio*):
    O du Wunderschöne Eh!

ISABELLA (*fröhlich*):
    Komm, mein Leben! komm, mein Herz!
    Komm zur Hochzeit, komm zum Scherz.

HANS WURST:
    Gehn wir lieber auf einmal
    Auf St. Marx, ins Narrn-Spital.
        (*Isabella nimmt Hans Wurst bey der Hand, und unter
        Springen trara, trara, ab mit Hans Wurst.*)[24]

The baroque figures of the earlier Jesuit drama reappear in Kurz
in their original allegoric form, but their previously awesome
aspect now becomes the object of Bernardon's contempt:

ALLE:
    Ach! wir sind schon alle hin,
    Der Teufel der ist los,
    Ich weiss nicht, wo ich bin,
    Die Angst ist gar zu gross.
        (*Fiametta kommt als Geist.*)

FIAMETTA:
    Ich bin Fiamettens Geist,
    Der euch die Strafe weist.
        (*Bernardon kommt auch als Geist.*)

25

   Und ich bin Bernardon,
   Der euch giebt jetzt den Lohn.[25]

This *Singspiel, Der neue krumme Teufel* (1752), with words by
Kurz and music by Joseph Haydn provided the theatre with a
general parody of Italian melodrama, and more specifically it
satirised the person of Afflisio, the Italian impresario of the
Kärntnerthortheater at that time, as a result of which the
operetta was banned, after two[26] or three[27] performances.

   Due to the success and appeal of the entertainment offered by
Stranitzky, Prehauser, Kurz, Weiskern and the lesser known
members of the *Stegreifensemble,* comedy, or to be more precise,
burlesque, had firmly, but, as it proved, not unshakably established itself in the residential theatre at the Kärntnerthor between
the years 1712 and 1750, to the almost entire exclusion of other
forms of drama. None of its offerings can be described in any
way as aesthetic or literary, indeed as Lady Mary Wortley
Montague reported in her letter to the Pope, dated September 14,
1716,[28] and as extant texts also show,[29] the general tone of the
theatre was occasionally little better than obscene, as might be
expected of a vigorous and popular enterprise. It is, however,
important in the history of German literature as a phenomenon
that did not remain docile beneath the autocratic sway of foreign
drama, but manipulated that material to its own ends. It imposed
upon it a criticism, which was not simply popular, but—what
was significant in that it provided something of a nursery for
the later growth of a national drama—one which was German.
The aristocracy with its private theatres had as yet kept its
mind largely closed to Germany's lack of a national drama,[30]
and it was particularly through the popular theatre, however
distasteful it might have been to the more privileged, that the
people of Vienna were brought to some awareness of this lack.
However, in the next two decades, even the popular theatre in
Vienna was, at least temporarily, to lose its place to foreign and
often second-rate dramatic values.

THE CONFLICT BETWEEN OLD VIENNESE POPULAR THEATRE AND LITERARY DRAMA IN THE KÄRNTNERTHORTHEATER

During the reign of Prehauser and the *Stegreifensemble* the popular theatre was to suffer considerably from a growing interest in Vienna in "regular" literary drama, and from the purists who demanded the expulsion of Hans Wurst from the German stage. Even in Stranitzky's day the banal antics of the popular comedian had been criticised. The *Parnassus Boicus,* a periodical founded in 1722 in Munich by E. Amort, A. Kandler and G. Hieber, bore witness to the transition from baroque to the new style of German literature and its items included a history of the German language by Hieber, written from the standpoint of purity and folk-content. Both Hieber's *Von der Poeterey* and Gottsched's later *Versuch einer kritischen Dichtkunst* strongly disapproved of Hans Wurst and the latter further recommended that the as yet immature German theatre should condescend to be guided by the rules and unities of French classical drama. As a result of this outlook and, subsequently, of the growing fame of the Neuber and Schönemann strolling companies who took up Gottsched's message of purgation, the Viennese audience began to look more favourably on literary drama. Thus from its pre-mière in 1747 *Vitichal und Dankwart, die alemannischen Brüder,* a literary product of the combined efforts of an actor, Weidner, who devised it, and of Krüger, who set it in verse, could enjoy considerable success.[1]

In Vienna a lively struggle ensued between the members of the *Stegreifensemble* and those who wished to establish a literary drama in the Kärntnerthortheater, and in 1749 Gottfried Heinrich Koch, an advocate of the latter, left the city, unable to withstand the fierce competition from the extempore theatre. In addition literary drama lost Gottlob Heydrich and Christiane Friedrich Lorenzin to the "bearers of the green hat"[2]. Not content with this, the latter company resorted to theatrical mis-representation in an attempt to denigrate its rivals still further:

> ... Sie führten unter dem Schein, als wären sie selbst da, in diesen Stücken zu spielen, Alzire auf ... Madame Nuth, eine Frau von 46 Jahren mit einem schwerfälligen Körper, machte die Alzire; Madame Schröter und Müller, jede ebenfalls über 40 Jahre alt, ihre beyden Vertrauten, Huber den Zamor, Schröter den Alvar und Mayberg den Montez. Man liess nach Gefallen aus, das Lernen zu ersparen, mit einem Worte, das Stück wurde vorsetz-lich verpfutscht.[3]

Especially active in ridiculing the products of the literary theatre were two leading members of the *Stegreifensemble*, Weiskern and Mayberg. Lessing's plays were performed together with Hans Wurst's follies, and Thomas Corneille's tragedy *Graf Essex* suffered from the intrusion of both Hans Wurst and Bernardon. The latter work nevertheless remained a success, being repeated fifteen times in the same year, and Koch had achieved moderate successes with *Oedipus* and *Zaïre* before he was driven from Vienna.

Another literary play *Iphigenie* withstood Weiskern's attacks and ran successfully until 1751, the year in which Freiherr von Lopresti, formerly director of the Italian Opera, became mana-ger of the German company. Under Lopresti the theatre included literary plays in its repertoire, translations from Goldoni and the tragedies of Corneille, which afforded the company greater finan-cial profit than burlesques. A tragedy was staged every Thurs-day and every three weeks a new tragedy was brought to the theatre. The literary play had won its place in the repertoire of the Kärntnerthortheater.

But as the infiltration of literary drama became more intense and its success more noticeable, Empress Maria Theresia sought to centralize the Court's power over the theatre and in 1751 she dismissed Lopresti and imposed a censorship. The Royal Imperial decree of February 11, 1752 stated:

> Die comödie solle keine andere compositionen spillen als die aus den französischen oder wälischen oder spanischen theatres her-kommen, alle hiesigen compositionen von Bernardon und andern völlig auffzuheben, wan aber einige gutte doch wären von weis-kern, sollen selbe ehender noch gelesen werden und keine

equivoques noch schmutzige Worte darinnen gestattet werden, auch denen comödianten ohne straffe nicht erlaubet werden sich selber zu gebrauchen.[4]

Punishments were announced for those who ignored the above decree and are noted in the *Wiener Hoftheateralmanach* of 1804. A first offence would be severely reprimanded, a second would entail fourteen days' arrest and a third, life imprisonment. Had the decree been effective, the Wiener *Volksstück* would no doubt have had its existence in Vienna effectively curtailed, for its message was clearly intended for the ears of all members of the *Stegreifensemble*. It further revealed the aristocracy's preference for a literary drama which was not German.

The censor, however, experienced some difficulty in performing his task, on account of the spontaneous, capricious humour of the *Volksstück*. That the decree failed in its aims is affirmed by Sonnenfels in his *Briefe über die Wienerische Schaubühne*, which appeared some time later in 1768:

> . . . und wovon die Polizey des Schauspiels dem öffentlichen Aergernisse vorzubauen, einige Strophen zu unterdrücken für notwendig hielt. Aber was nicht gedruckt werden sollte, warum hatte der Possenreisser das öffentlich auf den Brettern gesungen.[5]

The failure of the decree might also be attributed to the Empress's reluctance to enforce the severe punishments imposed, and certainly Franz Joseph later condoned the liberties of the popular theatre.

The *Stegreifensemble* responded immediately to the censorship and produced a flood of *Bernardoniaden, Hanswurstiaden*, and other burlesques, but the quantity belied the quality and subsequent reception. Joseph Huber's popular fool, Leopoldl, came into being at this time, and music and magic offered an additional attraction to the Viennese audience. The group was sorely beset, however, when the popular comedienne, Anna Maria Nuth, the portrayer of Colombine, died in 1754, for she had enjoyed such a degree of local fame that an audience had on one occasion demanded the return of its money after discovering that she was not to play on that particular night.

On May 14, 1752, a French company of actors had opened their season in the Burgtheater with a performance of Thomas Corneille's *Graf Essex*. As successful exponents of literary drama, the French actors were a serious threat to the further survival of the *Stegreifensemble* and the Wiener *Volksstück*. German literary drama, however, also suffered a setback at the hands of the French by losing the nobility of its audience to them. It was at this time that Maria Theresia decided to summon Karoline Neuber to Vienna, perhaps in an attempt to stimulate the cause of German literary drama, but little consolation was drawn from the venture. Karoline Neuber and her company had no success in the city when she came in 1753 and she therefore had to leave in the following year.

Changes now took place in both divisions of the Kärntnerthortheater. In 1759 the performances of new, literary plays increased in number, while the *Stegreifensemble* multiplied its output of "professional fools"; Durazzo, now impresario at the theatre, procured the services of the elder Stephanie, Kirchhof and Jacquet for 1760. In the same year Joseph Kurz, the creator of Bernardon, left the company for a time, and in April, Huber, originator of Leopoldl and, according to the *Wiener Hoftheateralmanach* of 1804, of *Zauberkomödie*, died. Despite the advent of Anton Brenner's Burlin the popularity of burlesques declined rapidly, and literary drama consolidated its position in the minds of a relatively better educated audience.

On November 3, 1761 the Kärntnerthortheater was burnt down, an event which necessitated the alternation of German and French companies in the Burgtheater. The former had often to appear in the grubby costumes of the latter, and the immediate comparison between the two brought discredit to both the German literary and popular theatre, the superiority of the French company being abundantly evident:

> Man setzte hiedurch das einheimische Schauspiel einem fremden nach, und die Nettigkeit, der Pomp, die pünktlichste Ordnung, welche bey den französischen Vorstellungen herrschte, thaten den deutschen Schauspielern in den Augen des Publikums gewaltigen Abbruch.[6]

On July 9, 1763, the Court Architect, Freyherr von Pacassi, had completed the new theatre, which was opened with one of Weiskern's occasional farces and followed by Philipp Hafner's *Die bürgerliche Dame*.[7]

Towards the end of 1763 the theatre engaged two more actors,

Friedrich Müller, who played the part of Sever in *Polyeucte*, and Christoph Gottlieb, who created Jakerle, another popular figure. Literary drama continued to win support and now a tragedy was performed every Thursday and a comedy every Tuesday, all other nights still being taken by burlesques. In 1764 Graf Sporck had the directorship of the theatre conferred upon him, Durazzo having been sent as ambassador to Venice. The voices of literary critics now began to grow more audible.[8] Christian Gottlob Klemm, later to become a teacher in the Imperial *Normalschule* when it was opened on January 2, 1771, after the Empress's reorganization of school management, denounced Hans Wurst, Burlin and Jakerl in his periodical, the *Moralische Wochenschrift*, and Sonnenfels was much of the same mind when he expressed his disgust at the idiotic farces of the popular stage in his *Letters* of 1768. Such were the pressures brought to bear that the most voluble of the defenders of extempore acting, Weiskern, was forced to "restrict his activities".

On the death of Franz Joseph in 1765 the French actors were dismissed and the theatre was let to Hilverding von Memen, who reopened it on the second day of Easter, 1766. Klemm, who had since become secretary, was sent to Leipzig to engage actors and playwrights, and was commissioned to pay 100 Gulden for a "large play" and 50 Gulden for a "small play". Kornelius von Ayrenhoff was now working to some effect on the side of literary drama. From information provided in the *Hoftheateralmanach* of 1804 and the Gotha *Theaterkalender* of 1779,[9] referring to the previous year, his tragedy *Hermann und Thusnelde* was performed on eight occasions in 1769, his three-act comedy *Der Postzug* nine times in the same year, and his tragedy *Aurelius* also met with considerable success. Nor did his productivity cease at this point for the almanac speaks of three tragedies and three comedies. The money which Ayrenhoff received for the acceptance of each third play, he gave to one of the actors or actresses.

But as yet the success of literary drama was by no means assured and the uncertainty about its future was further encouraged by an ominous lack of original plays. Hilverding wrote a few *Kinderkomödien* but these had little to offer of permanent value. The French plays which were available, were in the first place badly translated, and in the second, extremely undesirable because they had only recently been performed in Vienna by the French company. Hilverding's search for something new and literary was in vain and even if such material had been forthcoming, the theatre of literary drama was still suffering from the *Burleskanten,* who were unwilling to memorize their parts, and from a lack of actors other than those who were members of the *Stegreifensemble.* A constant threat to any hopes for a German national theatre was the unpatriotic longing of the aristocracy, who, as the almanac of 1804 reports, craved: ". . . französische Komödie, welche immer sein Lieblingsschauspiel gewesen war."[10] It was on such an avowal of duty towards the aristocracy that Afflisio, another Italian, was engaged as director of the theatre, replacing Hilverding. He promised "to establish once more a good French theatre". In 1768 Afflisio fulfilled his promise and rocked a somnolent German national theatre back on its heels by his declared policy. The almanac describes the effects almost tragically:

> Ohne Kenntnisse der deutschen Sprache, ohne Willen und Geschicklichkeit überliess sich Affligio blinden Führern, die ihm riethen, nur Possen zu geben, wenn er Nützen von seiner Unternehmung ziehen wollte. Er befolgte diesen Rath auf das pünktlichste, vernachlässigte das Nationaltheater gänzlich und verschwendete ungeheure Summen auf das französische Theater, auf die opera buffa, und die Ballete.[11]

In the Easter of 1769 Freyherr von Bender became manager of the German theatre and the French theatre remained under Afflisio with Heufelden as its director. Bender's intentions were to banish burlesque from the stage and to establish *ein studirtes gesittetes Theater.* He was not alone in his stand by this time and the Gotha *Theateralmanach* of 1776, referring to this year, provides evidence, in the form of a list of contemporary criticisms of the theatre, of more widespread support in the drive against the coarseness of the popular theatre,[12] although it ultimately attributes to Bender alone the privilege of having rid the German stage of the burlesque. The Gotha *Theaterkalender* of 1776 was not to know that Bender's success was only a temporary one. In the meantime actors competed keenly against each other and kept themselves in good physical condition so that they could stage two or three plays per week. The "good taste" prevailed. However the theatre was still not successful financially and had therefore to be returned to Afflisio after only six months.

The latter straightway demanded the return of the burlesque, but few actors in the theatre now wished to revert to them, particularly as their contracts with the management had been carefully phrased to discourage participation in burlesques and other *Stegreifspiele*. The *Stegreifensemble* itself by this time was in no position to enforce the revival of the burlesque, for it had recently had its talented membership greatly reduced. Anna Maria Nuth had died in 1754, Joseph Kurz had left the city in 1760, Mayberg and Schröter had died in 1761, Huber in 1760, and three more protagonists were to follow in rapid succession, Leinhaas in 1767, Weiskern in 1768 and Prehauser on January 29, 1769. Only Jackerle remained.

This impasse for Afflisio turned his attention to the Badner strolling company, which Menninger had recently brought to Vienna. It was hoped that, having already obtained permission to play in the suburbs, the company would agree to appear twice a week in the Kärntnerthortheater. Members of the latter theatre foresaw Afflisio's intentions to dismiss them and alternate with touring companies, and a play subsequently appeared in which the elder Stephanie, now a successful and respected member of the theatre, presented the dishonouring of the company and of its *Schauplatz*, and accordingly sought protection from the Imperial Court. The outcome of this was that the Court: ". . . allen fremden Truppen auf dem k.k. Theater zu spielen die Erlaubniss verweigert, und das Extemporiren untersagt wurde."[13] This was virtually the last nail in the coffin of the *Stegreifensemble*. Its last exponent, Joseph Kurz, who returned to Vienna in 1770, now had to write down his plays and *Singspiele* and submit them to the censor. His *La serva padrona, Die Herrschaftsküche* and *Die Weiber-und Bubenbataille* appeared at this time. But his popularity now diminished rapidly and the almanac of 1804 preferred to attribute this to the more discerning theatre-goers rather than to Kurz's advancing years, which was more widely accepted at the time. Kurz's career closed at the end of Fasching (pre-Lent Carnival) 1771 when his operetta *Die Judenhochzeit* was whistled off the stage.

The last Imperial pronouncement forced Afflisio to acknowledge the futility of persevering with the *Volksstück*, that is, the burlesque, and resign, and the genre found itself, of necessity, committed to an itinerant life once again, mostly to the strolling stage of the provinces, occasionally to the market-places and rudely-constructed huts in the suburbs. On the literary side the theatre continued to engage new actors, singers and directors. Hofschauspieler Müller travelled throughout Germany seeking to employ the best actors available.

Noverre, who soon gained a remarkable degree of popularity, was engaged as master of the ballet, and he, in turn, with the blessing of Joseph II, installed Johannes Böhm,[14] previously of the theatre in Brünn, with a view to his presenting German *Singspiele* alongside the ballet. Kohary, director of the theatre since 1770, found maintenance of Noverre's ballets increasingly costly, their lavish settings, the German and French plays and the *opera seria* and *buffa* involving a sum of 200,000 Gulden per annum. In 1772 he was forced to dismiss the French company and pay them 16,000 Gulden as their contract had not yet expired. By 1773 Kohary was even deeper in debt and in the following year Noverre had to be dismissed. The theatre's debts increased in 1775 and the audiences had dwindled hard upon the departure of the French company and Noverre.

In defiance of its financial position the theatre continued the struggle to realize its aims. It became the first theatre to offer monetary assistance in the form of prizes to those dramatic poets whose standards enabled them to create works deemed worthy of production by the company. Thus the theatre acknowledged the lack of literary plays in German and offered a practical remedy. The Gotha *Theaterkalender* of 1778 contains a copy of the advertisement which appeared on February 15 in the previous year.

Originalschauspiele für die deutsche Nation, Werke des ächten Genies, wo Natur und Kunst richtig verbunden sind und deren Verfasser nicht regellos umherschweifen, noch von willkürlichen Vorschriften sich im besten Dichterfluge hemmen lassen. Schauspiele dieser Art giebt es noch immer sehr wenige: deren Anzahl vermehrt zu wissen, ist ein Wunsch aller Freunde der deutschen Nationalschaubühne.

Die Kaiserl. Königl. Theatral-Hof-Direktion will nunmehr durch öffentliche Erklärung, alle dazu fähige Geister in Deutschland ermuntern, der Nationalbühne Ruhm befördern zu helfen; und wenn sie für Wien gute brauchbare Originalschauspiele liefern wollen, so sollen sie zur Vergeltung folgendes erhalten :

Für ein ungedrucktes Stück von gewöhnlicher Grösse, ganze Schauspiele, es sey ein Trauerspiel oder Lustspiel, die Einnahme, wie sie, nach dem gesetzten Preise, am Abende der dritten Vorstellung, baar eingeht, ohne den mindesten Abzug, ausgezahlt am nächst folgendem Tage. Kleinere Stücke von Wert können um die Hälfte geschätzt werden. Nur eine kleine Erinnerung, besonders für auswärtige Schriftsteller, deren Arbeiten uns bestimmt sind, dass ihr vornehmstes Augenmerk unser Publikum, hiesiger Ort, gegenwärtige Zeit seyn müsse. Was allgemein zu beobachten, wäre wohl überflüssig hier anzuführen.

Jeder Verfasser kann übrigens versichert seyn, dass die Annahme oder Verwerfung seines Stücks, ohne zu hoch gespannte Kritik, nur in Rücksicht auf unser Theater und Publikum geschehen soll; auch dass die Kayserl. Königl. Censur, mit nachsichtsvoller Billigkeit, ihren Anspruch zu thun, gewohnt ist.

An Stephanie den ältern, Regisseur des Nationaltheaters können die Manuscripte eingesandt werden, welcher allemal nach Monatsfrist, vom Tage des Empfangs angerechnet, entweder die Annahme versichern, oder das Manuscript zurückstellen wird. . .

The response to the appeal was that the theatre found itself with eighty-four new plays to judge, and the same *Theaterkalender* includes the list of prize-winners; on April 5, the younger Stephanie with *Der Unterschied bey Dienstbewerbungen*, a five-act comedy; on September 20, H. Richter with *Der Gläubiger*, a three-act comedy, and *Die Feldmühle*, a two-act comedy; on October 25, the Herzogl. Comm. Rath. Herr Schmidt with a five-act drama *Hermannide* and a two-act comedy *Wer ist in der Liebe unbeständig?* and towards the end of November young Lessing with a five-act comedy *Der Bankerottier*.[16]

The growing interest in a German national theatre had already been stimulated in 1776 by the co-regent, Joseph II, who had in that year once again thrown open the stage of the Kärntnerthortheater to all strolling companies, foreign or native.[17] Having thus given the popular theatre its freedom, he was to pursue his policy further two years later when he moved the German company of actors from the Kärntnerthortheater into the Burgtheater and declared the latter the *Hof- und Nationaltheater*. In the same year and in the same theatre he initiated the *Teutsches Nationalsingspiel*.

However positive these moves might have seemed, they were prompted by certain destructive urges on Joseph's part. With patriotic fervour he had decided to destroy the French theatre in Vienna, mainly because it was French, but also because the Viennese nobility derived enjoyment from it. This was in accordance with his policy of removing undeserved privileges from the nobility in an attempt to reimburse the underprivileged classes. Hitherto the theatre had been supported by the proceeds from legalized gambling, each faro bank paying ten ducats, but now Joseph saw to it that gambling was forbidden. Having ruined the French theatre financially, he placed it under the jurisdiction of the Court. It was officially designated the German National Theatre and the change was accompanied by a reduction in the price of seats.[18]

But the Imperial Court and the theatre became indissoluble and with that the character of the Burgtheater was determined for some years to come. The Emperor often visited the theatre and attended rehearsals, decisions taken by the production committee had to be ratified by the *Hofdirektion*, and the *Hoftheateralmanach* of 1804 remarks that the nobility always came in full attendance to their German stage. The actors did not become *deutsche Schauspieler* but remained *Hofschauspieler* and the theatre was managed by the Court Chamberlain. Popular theatre was now the affair of the strolling companies, of Vienna's surburban, and sometimes, amateur theatres, while German literary drama remained to a great extent the concern of an aristocratic society.

PHILIPP HAFNER AND THE GROWTH OF
POPULAR VIENNESE TRADITIONS

In the three volumes of Hafner's *Gesammelte Schriften*, published in Vienna in 1812, the editor, Joseph Sonnleithner, recorded a number of incidents from Hafner's life, which bore witness to his irrepressible spirit. It was only towards the end of a very short life that Hafner, who died at the age of 33, dedicated himself to the service of the theatre. This was in 1763, but even before that time his forceful personality made itself felt in the private circumstances illustrated by several of the anecdotes, and also in his early profession as a lawyer:

> Der Mann, welcher bey dem Stadtgerichte die Schreibmaterialen in Verwahrung hatte, war mit dem Papiere sehr karg. Hafner sollte das erste Verhör eines Menschen, der bey dem Gericht eingebracht worden war, aufnehmen, schickte um Papier, und erhielt keines. Ohne sich lang zu bedenken, nahm er das Verhör vor, schrieb die Aussage mit Kreide auf den Tisch, und da die Verhöre dem Stadtrichter vorgelegt werden sollten, liess er den Tisch zu ihm tragen. Als er zur Rede gestellt wurde, erwiederte er, dass er es für eine Gewissenssache gehalten habe, die Verhaftung eines Menschen, der doch unschuldig seyn konnte, des Papiergeitzes wegen um einen Tag zu verlängern.[1]

Hafner at heart was a dramatist of the popular stage, as the spirit behind his comedies shows and as he himself demonstrates in a letter addressed to a *Kunsterfahrener Herr*, presumably Durazzo: "Für die studierten und regelmässigen Stücke bin ich eben nicht geboren worden, aber für das Aufgeweckte, Extemporirte bin ich (hohl mich Apollo!) geschaffen. . ."[2] His later comedies on the other hand illustrated his faith in the greater durability of literary drama, yet even here Sonnleithner takes care to point out that Hafner allowed the comedy of the *Stegreifensemble* freedom within his play. His later comedies are neater in form, more consistent and mature in the presentation of character and of comedy, and differ from his early plays in that they become comedies of character in the manner of Molière, rather than comedies of situation in the manner of the *commedia dell' arte* and the popular theatre of the strolling companies. Hafner's productivity was limited to the last two years of his life, 1763 and 1764. But he is important in the development of the Old Viennese Popular Theatre, not simply as its only literary writer at the time, but as one who—in his refinement of plots from the *commedia* and adaptation of plots from Molière—established for the theatre a series of literary models, colourful theatrical situations, local Viennese caricatures and comic business, which formed the basis for the further growth of a popular tradition.

Of Hafner's earlier plays *Der alte Odoardo*[3] and *Der geplagte Odoardo*[4] have little more to offer than a comedy along the traditional lines of the typical plot of the *commedia*, where the tyrannical father-figure, Odoardo, is sorely taxed to save his beautiful daughter, Isabella, from the amorous advances of one, or more, suitors. In the former play there is only one suitor for the daughter's hand and that is Leander. There is but one rival, Anselmo, and he is the old man, whom, for reasons of finance, Odoardo would have his daughter marry. Scapin is the servant of Odoardo and Hans Wurst serves the hero, Leander.

By this time magic was part of the tradition of the popular theatre, and Hafner reveals the careless composition of this, his first play, by leaving the entire dénouement of the plot in the hands of the magician, his reasons for this attitude being: ". . . mir fällt itzt nicht gleich eine Ursach bey, und vorhin hab ich ungefähr darauf vergessen."[5] His second play is a distinct improvement and already shows signs of Hafner's future maturity as a dramatic writer. The characterisation is nevertheless still inconsistent and its demands are sacrificed to the demands of situation. Thus it is felt that Crispin's anger with his master, Baron Pappendeckel, subsides because it is essential to the plot that he delivers the baron's letter to Mitzerl.[6] There are, however, several instances in the play of effective farce, and in the following extract Casperl obeys to the letter his master's injunction that he should admit to the house neither Tom, Dick nor Harry:

CASPERL (*hält ihn ab*): Wohin? Zurück da! Wohin?

BARON PAPPENDECKEL: In das Haus dahier will ich hineingehen.

CASPERL: Ist der Herr der Paul?

BARON PAPPENDECKEL: Ich bin der, der ich bin, was haht Ihr darnach zu fragen?

CASPERL: Ich hab stark danach zu fragen, denn ich muss wissen, ob der Herr der Paul ist?

BARON PAPPENDECKEL (*vor sich*): Es scheint mir, als ob der Kerl den Befehl hatte, Niemanden ausser einen sichern Paul in das Haus zu lassen, allein ich will dem dummen Teufel schon durch den Sinn fahren. (*Zu Casperl.*) Nu! wenn Ihr es doch wissen müsst, so will ich es euch sagen; ja! ich bin der Paul!

CASPERL (*lacht*): Ja! no so geh der Herr nur seinen Weg, der Herr kommt nicht hinein.

BARON PAPPENDECKEL: Und warum soll ich nicht hineinkommen?

CASPERL: Weder der Peter noch der Paul kommt hinein.

BARON PAPPENDECKEL (*vor sich*): Je, was Teufel! Da bin ich schön angekommen! Was woll ich machen? (*Zu Casperl.*) Guter Freund! wenn Ihr mich in das Haus lasst, so schenk ich Euch sechs Ducaten.

CASPERL (*weint*): Gütiger Himmel, warum hast Du einen so generosen Herrn lassen zu einem Paul werden?[7]

When Hafner's *Megära, die förchterliche Hexe*[8] was performed in Pacassi's reconstructed Kärntnerthortheater in 1763, it met with immediate and lasting success. Within the course of its plot it included the elements of music and magic, which had already become inherent parts of the traditional comedy of the popular theatre, and posterity has since seen fit to designate the play a *Zaubersingspiel*, although its author was quite content with a mere title and did not attempt to specify genre.

The plot is a variation on the theme of *Der alte Odoardo* and *Der geplagte Odoardo* with the hero, Leander, and the heroine, Angela, enjoying the additional support of a magic guardian, Megära, and Odoardo in part two, the similar support of the wizard, Orkamiastes. There is some doubt as to the moral function of these magic powers, as it is Megära's declared duty to defend those who suffer from the tyranny of obstinate fathers,[9] and it is the similar obligation of Orkamiastes to protect the oppressed,[10] yet both powers are diametrically opposed to

39

each other as the plot runs its course. It is no easy matter to distinguish between good and evil in the affairs of magic, and although Part One has great sympathy with Megära's cause, the second part bears witness to a decided change of heart as Orkamiastes grows more active in the pursuit of justice. Inevitably of course, remaining completely within the bounds of the popular theatre, the play ends with the complete reconciliation of all parties, human and magical, a solution which is foretold in the title of Part Two: *Der förchterlichen Hexe Megära, Zweyter Theil. Unter dem Titel: die in eine dauerhafte Freundschaft sich verwandelnde Rache* (. . . Revenge transformed into lasting Friendship.) The finale of the play, however, does not conform completely to the demands of popular theatre, for Leander, in a fit of moral indignation at the momentary perfidy of his beloved in Part One, when she fell a victim to Gassbiegel's advances, stoutly maintains that infidelity is too strong an insult to be washed away by tears.[11] Friendship is the compromise.

The power of magic in *Megära* is not absolute and is demonstrated merely as an accessory of a traditional plot. Odoardo, for instance, succeeds in shooting down the "flying-cloud"; the wizard Orkamiastes is somewhat degraded when he has to grapple physically with Leander before he can fling him down into Hell; and even the original magician Schlickziroschurakas is governed by the laws of mortality and dies. Nor does Megära hold herself aloof from involvements with humans and in Part Two she even becomes emotionally involved in the plot. Nor is the rule of magic seen as interminable for only six years remain of the ninety-year contract with Pluto, and in the words of Orkamiastes: ". . . alsdann ist die Periode der Hexerey vorüber."[12]

In addition to its integral purpose in the plot, magic serves the ends of the popular theatre by attracting the audience visually. The construction and employment of the "flying-cloud" and the finale of the first part, where Odoardo, Anselmo and Riepel are left hanging from a chandelier with lights shining on their heads, arms and feet, ask little of stage mechanicians who can successfully present Megära's conjuration of the spirits in Act 1:

ARIA 1

Megära

Nehmt die unumschränkte Macht
Meiner Künste wohl in Acht!

40

Lasst Euch unerschrocken sehen!
Denn Euch soll kein Leid geschehen;
Wenn gleich alles kracht und bricht,
So bleibt ruhig, zittert nicht.
(Sie macht mit dem Stabe verschiedene Kreise in der Luft, und
auf der Erde.)
Pluto, Charon, Phlegeton,
Lethe, Stix, und Acheron,
Tantalus, und Radamas,
Sisiphus, und Salzverkass,
Teufeln, Furien der Höllen,
Hört mein ernstliches Befehlen,
Seyd zu meinem Wink bereit!
(Man höret ein erschröckliches Geschrey.)
Hört wie ihr Geschwader schreyt!
(Zu Hw. und Leander.)
Die Unmöglichkeit der Sachen,
Kann ich öfters möglich machen;
Mit dem Stab befehl ich nur,
Gleich gehorcht mir die Natur.
Ich darf einmahl nur gebieten,
Alsbald muss das Wasser wüthen,
(Der Fluss fängt an zu wellen.)
Alsbald thürmen sich im Lauf,
Die sonst sanfte Wellen auf;
Kaum wird es von mir befohlen,
So hört man den Donner rollen,
(Es kommen Wolken, welche die Sonne verfinstern, wobey es
donnert und blitzt.)
So entzündet sich der Blitz,
So verschwindt der Sonne Hitz.
Bäume kann ich auch beleben;
(Die an dem Gestad stehende Bäume bewegen sich.)
Berge müssen Feuer geben,
(Der hinter dem Wasser stehende Berg speyt Feuer.)
Und ein beseelter Stein,
Muss ein Frauenzimmer seyn.
(Der an dem Wasser stehende kleine Felsen, verkehrt sich in
ein Frauenzimmer.)
An der Treue meiner Teufeln,
Dürft Ihr keinesweges zweifeln;
(Es kommen von beyden Seiten Teufeln von der Erde, welche
einander umfangen, mitten kommt der Tod aus der Erde.)

Seht, sogar der schlaue Tod
Kommt, und ehret mein Geboth.
Meine wohl gebauten Riesen
Hab ich euch noch nicht gewiesen.
  (*Es kommen zwey Riesen.*)
Habt Ihr sie genau betracht?
Sagt! Sind sie nicht schön gemacht?
Gleichfalls muss meine Zwergen
Evrer Neugier nicht verbergen;
Von den Plagen müssen zween
Stäts an meiner Tafel stehn.
  (*Es kommen vier hässliche Zwergen.*)
Bären, Tyger, Löwen, Drachen.
Weiss ich Lämmern gleich zu machen,
  (*Es kommen fliegende Drachen, wie auch einige kriechende
  Thiere, welche sich der Zauberinn zu Füssen legen.*)
Seht, wie sanft sie ruhen hier!
O! die allerliebsten Thier! (*sie streichelt die Thiere.*)
  (*Zu Leander und Hw.*)
Nun habt Ihr es schon gesehen,
Was durch meine Macht geschehen,
Drum Gespenster, weicht zurück!
Fort in einem Augenblick!
  (*Alle Gespenster entfernen sich, die Riesen gehen ab, die
  Zwerge auch, die Thiere kriechen, die Teufel umfangen sich
  wieder, und verschwinden, wie der Tod unter Feuer, die
  Drachen fliegen ab, die Wetterwolken verziehen sich, es hört
  auf zu donnern, und zu blitzen, die Sonne scheint wieder, das
  Frauenzimmer verwandelt sich wieder in einen Felsen, die Wel-
  len hören auf sich zu thürmen.*)
Du Natur! lass dich nun wieder
In die alte Ruhe nieder!
Thue meinem Wink genug,
Ohne mindesten Verzug.
  (*Zu Hw. und Leander.*)
Nu! wie gefallen Euch diese Kleinigkeiten?[13]

Part Two of *Megära*, whilst not as effective as the first part,
for it is felt on several occasions that certain scenes and personalities are introduced merely to fill out what is essentially a weak
plot, is nevertheless of some interest in that it heralds the later
development of a particular genre of Viennese popular theatre
known as *Lokalstück*, which won for itself a degree of fame in

Marinelli's Leopoldstadttheater after 1781, in Schikaneder's Freihaustheater after 1791 and in the latter's hands and those of Raimund and Nestroy achieved individual distinction as a genre in its own right. The *Lokalstück*, as its name suggests, is concerned essentially with the presentation of local colour, Vienna in this case. Thus a number of city characters, or to be more precise, caricatures, are introduced in the second part: the schoolmaster, who is caricatured by an abundance of foreign vocabulary, which he frequently misuses, the judge likewise by a deferential "Vor Ihnen zu reden", Odoardo's cousin Herr von Nigewitz, the latter's servant, Ramamperl, and a doctor by the name of Weinstein, who attends Odoardo and presents a caricature of a contemporary quack. His farcical prescriptions and his completely irresponsible attitude in diagnosing Odoardo's ailment are a constant reminder of Fuchsmundi's similarly light-hearted treatment in Stranitzky's *Ollapatrida* of 1711[14] of a topic which in reality offered untold hardship to the citizens of eighteenth century Vienna. Weinstein allows a little more of what were then Viennese drinking habits to be revealed in his speech:

> Sie können sichs leicht auswendig merken, ich brauche lauter Hausmittel. Lassen Sie sich einen scabiosen Tee mit Wanzen und Rosoli Milchraum* machen, der kühlt Sie ab und wird Ihnen ein wenig die Natur ändern, er ist sonst eine Herzstärk** für die verzweifelten Narren, und wird Ihnen darauf nicht besser, so krepiren Sie ins Himmels Nahmen alle beyde.[15]

The editor of Hafner's collected works, Joseph Sonnleithner, here adds two footnotes to explain two of the terms mentioned in the above passage, a practice in which he indulges throughout the collection and which, in itself, if a little academically, enriches the local interest of Hafner's plays. For "Milchraum" he adds: "Milchraum für Milchrahm; der gemeinste Oesterreicher sagt Müliram, mit hohem A." and for "Herzstärk": "Herzstärk für Herzstärkung braucht Hafner hier wahrscheinlich nur zum Scherz, um auf die Stärke anzuspielen; Doctor Weinstein verordnet gleichsam einen Herzkleister." Within the context of the play are countless other references to the city and its life, such as the asylum at St. Marx, the currency and cost of living and the diurnal habits of tea- and coffee-drinking, which intensify the atmosphere of local colour and continue the popular associations of the theatre.

The popular comedians, represented in this play by Hans Wurst, Leander's servant, Colombine, Angela's maid, and Riepel, Odoardo's domestic servant, who is distinguished from Hans Wurst by his greater inexperience and naïvety, continue within the tradition of Hafner's two earlier plays. Hans Wurst displays his customary versatility by appearing under various disguises which help him to deceive Odoardo and his followers. He is very convincing as an undertaker and parody is inferred by the humour of his funereal incantation, his tone assuming the melancholy solemnity of the poetry of the baroque age. Yet the comedy of the situation is readily apparent as the melodrama is merely pretended:

> (*Zu Col.*) Was weinen Sie mein Kind! wir sind zum Tod geboren!
> (*Zu den beyden Alten auf sie deutend.*) der morgen, jener heut, der Tod bleibt keinem aus.
>> Die Welt ist uns ja nur zur Marter auserkohren,
>> Der Leib ist unsrer Seel nichts als ein Krankenhaus,
>> Und darum wünsch ich auch die Ehre bald zu haben,
>> Mit meiner eignen Hand Sie beyde zu begraben.
>> (*Geht ernsthaft ab.*)[16]

The audience knows full well that neither Leander nor Hans Wurst is dead, but Colombine, Odoardo and Anselmo do not, and are so much beguiled by the undertaker that they display their genuine regrets at the supposed death of their antagonists in the intrigue. Ironically, for Odoardo does not know of the many parts which Hans Wurst yet has to play, he adds: "Der Kerl ist zugleich Leichenbitter, Todtengräber, und Poet". ("The fellow is a mourner, grave digger and poet all at once"). His other three parts are as baker, in which rôle he sings the song "Ein Bäck ist halt ein ganzer Mann. . ." ("A baker is a proper man. . .") innkeeper and lacquey, of which each impersonation reflects a measure of caricature, but where he responds solely to the stimuli of situation and not to the inward demands of character.

The function of Odoardo, Anselmo, Leander and Angela in the play strongly recalls the *commedia dell' arte*, but their characters are much more individual in Hafner than were the

44

stock-characters of the Italian company. The sub-title of the second part of *Megära*: . . . *die in eine dauerhafte Freundschaft sich verwandelnde Rache* suggests the obligations of the Viennese popular theatre of the 60's to human relationships and moral problems, and thirty years later in *The Magic Flute*, the hero Tamino, was to be similarly upbraided by the priest for his foolish desire for revenge, as Mozart's opera further established its link with popular tradition. Perhaps significantly, Odoardo ultimately relinquishes his tyrannical hold over his daughter and bows with good grace before the demands of the popular theatre for a general reconciliation of all opposing parties. Almost realistically, Odoarda acts sometimes from good and sometimes from bad motives. In his own way he is very concerned about his daughter's misery, when she believes that Leander is dead, yet on the other hand, he can only interpret Leander's death in terms of his own advantage. His obstinacy gives him courage in the face of danger, but his miserliness limits his vision. Leander is a noble-minded and sentimental suicide, whose character suffers the misfortune of being subjected, in conformity to the demands of popular theatre, to the comedy of Hans Wurst, and whose intended act of self-destruction lacks the true conviction of a lover's despair and therefore gives rise to the thought that this theatrical incident was included merely because it provided a most opportune entry for the witch, Megära:

LEAN.: . . . Ich kenn den Eigensinn und den Geiz des Odoardo, und da ich meine Angela nicht zur Frau bekommen kann, so soll sie durch meinen Tod erfahren, wie zärtlich ich sie geliebt hab, und Du wirst mir Gesellschaft im Tod leisten, denn ich muss einen Bedienten bey mir haben.

HW.: Nehmen Sie sich derweil in der andern Welt einen Lehnlaquey auf, bis ich ohne diess einmal nachkomm.

LEAN.: Nein, Du musst mit mir sterben, bedenk einmahl die Ehre, die wir von diesem Tod haben! Die Welt wird uns unter die Helden zählen.

HW.: Es wird mir lieber, die Welt zählet mich unter die lebendigen Hienzen, als unter todten Helden.

LEAN.: Du Zaghafter, Du musst ja ohne diess einmahl sterben. Also, mache fort, oder ich schiess Dir die Seele beym Ellenbogen heraus.

HW. (*voller Angst*): Potz tausend Fickerment, das ist ja doch

45

nicht erlaubt, einen Menschen mit Gewalt aus Lieb zum Sterben zwingen! Das ist ja doch nicht erhört worden!

LEAN.: Schweig, und gib acht, bleib auf Deinem Posto, nimm die Pistole und ziehl auf mich, alsdenn fange an zu zählen 1, 2, 3, und sobald Du drey sagst, so schiesst Du auf mich, und ich werde Dich a Tempo über den Haufen schiessen.

HW. (*stellt sich in furchtsame Positur, und fängt an eines zu zählen.*)

LEAN.: Halt ein! Bevor ich sterbe, muss ich noch in dieser Einöde einige Worte meiner angebetheten Angela schenken. Du kannst ein gleiches deiner Colombina zu Ehren thun. Angebethete Angela! . . .

HW.: Verfluchte Colombina! . . .

LEAN.: Weil ich in meinem Leben Dich nicht besitzen kann. . .

HW.: Ich wollt, dass ich Dich in meinem Leben nicht gesehen hätt, aber weil ich Dich gesehen hab. . .

LEAN.: So will ich aus Treue für Dich, weil Dich in eines andern Armen zu sehen mir unmöglich ist. . .

HW.: So muss ich schandenhalber mit meinem rasenden Herrn. . .

LEAN.: Meinen Geist aufgeben.

HW.: Meinen Geist erschiessen lassen.

LEAN. (*zu* HW.): Nun mache fort und commandire.

HW. (*in seiner lächerlichen Positur fängt immer an 1, 2, zu zählen, doch anstatt auf 3 zu kommen, fängt er allzeit wieder 1 an, oder zählt 4, 5, statt 3.*)

LEAN:. Schweig still! Weil ich sehe, dass Du ein zaghafter Narr bist, so werde ich das Commando führen.

HW. (*fängt an zu zittern*): Jetzt ists aus.

LEAN.: Gib acht, und sobald ich drey sage, so schiess auf mich: 1, 2, 3. (*Er schiesst los. HW. lässt bey dem Wort drey die Pistolen fallen, bevor Leander noch losgedruckt hat und fällt unter grossem Geschrey auf die Erde; zugleich eröffnet sich die auf der Seite an dem Gestad stehende grosse Felsen, welche sich in ein Zauberkabinett verwandelt.*)[17]

The first entry of the Queen of Night in *The Magic Flute*, when it appeared in September 1791, is in visual terms an almost exact reproduction of Megära's first entry. Actual terminology, of course, differs, but the picture is the same: "Die Berge teilen sich auseinander und das Theater verwandelt sich in ein prächtiges Gemach."[18] The suicide scene likewise was a common event on the popular stage and in *The Magic Flute*, Papageno performs a similar ceremony of numbers in Act II, sc. xxix, when he threatens to hang himself should no-one answer his mating-call:

> . . . Keine hört mich, alles stille! (*Sieht sich um.*)
> Also ist es euer Wille?
> Papageno, frisch hinauf!
> Ende deinen Lebenslauf! (*Sieht sich um.*)
> Nun, ich warte noch, es sei,
> Bis man zählet: Eins, zwei, drei. (*Pfeift.*)
> Eins! (*Sieht sich um, pfeift.*)
> Zwei! (*Sieht sich um.*)
> Zwei ist schon vorbei. (*Pfeift.*)
> Drei! (*Sieht sich um.*)
> Nun, wohlan, es bleibt dabei. . .[19]

Of course, the three genii manage to stay his hand, and, in fact, none of the suicide incidents on the popular stage ever ends tragically, unless pure parody is intended as in Hafner's *Eva-kathel und Schnudi*.[20] In this instance Papageno has chosen to leave the world with the aid of a rope, the same instrument of death which Anton Brenner's popular comedian Burlin came near to using in Hafner's play *Etwas zum Lachen im Fasching*.

The characterization of the heroine, Angela, is perhaps more realistic than would be normally expected of a merely popular playwright, where the custom was to romanticise the young couple in ideal terms. She suffers an obvious fall from this traditional grace, when she surrenders to the amorous advances of one Gassbiegel, really Megära in disguise, and it was for this reason that Leander would not forgive her perfidy at the end of the play. He, of course, remains the idealist in his lack of compromise. What is more interesting than their mutual relationship is the skilful manner in which Hafner so prepares the character of his heroine, that her downfall, though it be of a temporary nature, is not unexpected. This is executed by a subtle disclosure of the insincerity of her love beforehand, and of the wavering of her heart:

> . . . es ist zwar gewiss, dass der Leander mir allgemach etwas abhold zu werden anfängt, allein daran ist nicht so viel mein wankendes Herze, als die vielen Hindernissen dieser Liebe . . . Ursach.[21]

Clearly her love is one which takes and possesses and gives nothing in return. It is not the *amour de sacrifice* which one would ideally expect of the popular heroine, for what really upsets her about Leander's suicide, is not sadness at his death, but annoyance at not being any longer able to possess him completely and at his failure to free her from the clutches of her tyrannical father:

> ... bey dem ersten Anblicke bin ich dein gewesen, nur du warst allzu grausam gegen mich, dass du mir vielleicht durch eine unüberlegte That das Vergnügen, dich ewig zu besitzen, entzogen hast, da uns doch beyde eine schnelle Flucht von einem tyrannischen Vater befreyen, und dabey glücklich hätte machen können...[22]

Her effusive praise of Leander's portrait and the lavish kiss she bestows upon it, together with the pride she feels in her love and which is manifest in the same speech, condemn her affection as affectation:

> O meine liebe Colombina! Mein Herz ist voller Angst, was Leander auf den überschickten Brief vorgenommen, ob er mich bey meinem Herrn Vater zur Ehe begehrt, oder mein Vater mich ihm versaget; allein es koste, was es wolle, so muss ich Leandern besitzen; ohne ihn ist mir mein Leben zuwider, an ihm ganz allein finde ich alle jene Eigenschaften, die mein Herz vergnügen können. Betrachte einmahl sein Portrait, er ist eben nicht der schönste, aber er hat so ein gewisses Etwas, das fast alle Frauenzimmer reizen muss; siehst du sein Aug, wie verliebt, und zugleich, wie ernsthaft es ist, o das schöne Aug! (*Sie küsst das Portrait*). [23]

This is not only the manipulation of what became a traditional piece of stage-property in the popular theatre, namely the portrait, but it is deliberately integrated into the course of the plot to reveal the limitations of the heroine's love for the hero. Angela already reflects the class-conscious female of Viennese society and is beginning to assert her authority and add colour to the previously wan and spineless victim of a tyrannical father and an ardent lover. She finds satisfaction, to a degree, in the knowledge that she is loved. Happy in her megalomania she readily believes that Leander has committed suicide for her sake and even upbraids him for having thus abandoned her to the whims of her father. Even her compensatory attempt at suicide exists only fleetingly in her mind and does not have the compulsion of sincerity. On account of this shading, Leander's moralizing attitude at the end of the play is not unacceptable.

The play which Sonnleithner places last in the collected works of Hafner, *Evakathel und Schnudi*,[24] although it is designated tragi-comedy, is in effect parody, and in the nature of its comedy, which is of situation and not of character, would appear to belong to the early plays of Hafner. Sonnleithner refers to it as one of the earliest parodies in German literature, and it is clear in the course of the two acts of the play, that Hafner is guying the traditional plot which he himself inherited from the *commedia dell' arte* and of which he made use in the majority of the plays in his collected works. The comedy is present in the several manifestations of local colour, in the placing of popular and vulgar terminology in the mouths of high-born persons, and in giving the latter such colourful names as Pamstig, Evakathel, Schnudi, Diedeltapp and Schnackerl, each of which is explained in detail by the editor's footnotes.[25] Anachronisms are introduced to further the ends of comedy, when Pamstig bids his daughter to do some darning while he receives Schnudi's ambassador, and in the following scene Diedeltapp speaks of powder, lead, sabres and grenades. The use of verse has a similar humorous effect:

PAMSTIG:
Dein Bitten ist umsonst; steh auf, sonst kriegst Du Flaschen!
EVAKATHEL:
Die Deichsels Liebe brennt mein Herz zu Staub und Aschen;
    Herr Vater, ach!——
PAMSTIG:
Schweig still! Ich nehm Dich sonst beym Schopf.
EVAKATHEL:
Prinz Schnudi sey mein Mann——
PAMSTIG:
Der Lienel?
EVAKATHEL (*steht auf*):
Sey kein Knopf![26]

The climax of the parody of the traditional plot indicates the tragedy, which might ensue, if the father-figure, in this case Pamstig, were to remain completely obdurate and refuse to be reconciled to the idea of his daughter's marrying for love. Pamstig is killed for his obstinacy by his would-be son-in-law,

Schnudi, after a period of hair-pulling. On hearing the news of her father's death, Evakathel commits suicide with a pocket-knife, and, witnessing this act, Schnudi likewise expires after eating a bag of poisoned sweets. Schnudi's gruesome attempt to exculpate himself before Evakathel, when he walks on stage bearing her father's head aloft, and at the same time gives his apologies, is one of the most glaring instances of parody in the whole play:

SCHNUDI *(mit dem Kopfe des Tartarchens.)* :
   . . . Hör meine Unschuld doch ! Ich weiss, dass ich gefehlet,
   Und wider dein Geboth den Vater hab entseelet;
   Allein die Noth zwang mich, dass ich es so gemacht;
   Hätt ich ihn nicht gestutzt, hätte er mich umgebracht. . .[27]

Previous to this incident Evakathel expresses her appreciation of the impending tragedy in poetic terms: "Nur der den andern stürzt, macht sich zu meinem Feind". ("Only he who fells the other becomes my enemy"). But it is her horror on discovering that she still loves her father's murderer which motivates her suicide:

   Die Neigung gegen ihn ist noch, wie vor, zu heftig,
   Und meine Macht die Glut zu dämpfen, bleibt unkräftig;
   Drum straf ich das an mir, was ich an ihm nicht kann,
   Und weil ich ihn nicht krieg, so sterb ich ohne Mann.[28]

Both hero and heroine die in the conventional operatic manner, Schnudi, giving musical, and farcical, expression to his sufferings of the moment:

SCHNUDI :
   Ihr Freunde—Auweh zwick ! Lebt—wohl ! Auweh ich sterbe !
   Ach helfet !—Auweh zwick !—Ich berste, ich verderbe !
   Ach Feuer !—Auweh zwick !—Bringt Wasser ! Auweh zwick !
   Der Schmerzen—Auweh zwick !—steigt jeden Augenblick.
   Das Gift macht—Auweh zwick !—mir Quaal, es zerrt, es rennet.
   Der Magen—Auweh zwick !—wird durch und durch gebrennet !
   Prinzessinn !—Auweh zwick ! ich sterb—
     (Er fällt zu Boden und stirbt.)[29]

The form of the musical commentary on the deaths of the prince and princess is itself part of the parody for the two items are sung "Im Ton eines Steyrischen Tanzes", ("To the tune of a

Styrian dance".) and the editor equates the Styrian dance with the waltz, the former being merely an older term for the same thing.

In his comedy *Der Furchtsame*,[30] Hafner succeeds in adding a degree of literary distinction to his work, for now the comic concern of the play is not centred solely around the comedy of situation or of caricature, but reveals the beginnings of his interest in the comedy of character. Thus, in the manner of Molière, an individual becomes more important than the outcome of the plot, or its inherent incidents and its final reconciliation scenes. There is no magic in this play, but a kindred superstition, a belief in ghosts, is present in the main character, the father-figure, Hasenkopf. Significantly, the latter's credulity is part of his character and the figments of his imagination are never interpreted visually by the stage mechanicians. The editor notes that, at a time when mediaeval superstition was still in the process of being dispersed by the gathering forces of enlightenment, Hafner did not venture to commit himself on this topical issue,[31] but perhaps the mere name Hasenkopf (hare-brain) indicates the author's penchant. Due to the absence of technical machinery in the play, the human element assumes greater importance than hitherto in Hafner.

The outline of the plot is essentially that of *Megära* and of Hafner's earlier plays, but the treatment of individual characters has matured. Herr von Hasenkopf fulfils the same function as he did previously, but with a warmth which is out of keeping with what was his traditional rôle. At the same time the miserliness of the earlier father-figure, Odoardo, diminishes, for he has troubles other than financial ones. Even in his superstition though, he shows a genuine concern for the safety and well-being of the other parties in the intrigue, and with hardly even a show of reluctance he forgives all transgressions against his person at the end of the play. It is not his tyrannic authority, but true paternal concern for his daughter which motivates his traditional desire for a good marriage. With all his humanity, he is nevertheless unshakeable in his belief in ghosts, and neither Henriette, his daughter, nor Alkantor, his close friend, can assuage his fear as they appeal to his reason. Hafner depicts the old man's fanatical insistence on the veracity of his beliefs very convincingly:

"Ja?—Beym Henker! ich werde wohl noch einen Hund von der Klage zu unterscheiden wissen."[32]

Despite the traditional impatience with an obstinate father, Henriette remains kindly disposed towards him on the whole. She is not blemished with Angela's infidelity in *Megära*, but neither is she above showing a certain amount of ingratitude to her father. Almost unemotionally she gives voice to her desire to be liberated from him:

"... Wie glücklich werde ich seyn,wenn mich Valer heute Nacht von meinem wahnwitzigen Vater befreyen wird. . ."[33]

She is endowed with a great deal of common sense and sees her father's superstitions merely as products of his sick imagination. Similarly, at the end of the play, after the startling revelation that her lover, Valer, is in fact her brother, her ready and reasonable adaptability enables her to assimilate the situation quickly in its new perspective and rejoice at the discovery of her long-lost brother.

Hafner's greater maturity in this play is manifest throughout. The hero has developed so much beyond Leander in stature, that even when he is the subject of farce, he retaliates in character and angrily rebukes Hans Wurst, who plays his traditional rôle as companion and servant to the hero, for his effrontery. In the following extract Hans Wurst has just received a box on the ears from his counterpart, Lisette:

HANS WURST (*allein, höchst erzürnt*): Fourireschützen sakrament! Mir unschuldiger Weise eine Maulschelle zu geben? Die Maulschelle soll auf meinem Gesichte nicht sitzen bleiben! die muss herab. (*Er nimmt ein Schnupftuch aus dem Schubsacke, legt es auf die Erde, kniet nieder, und wischt eine Weile, als ob er die Ohrfeige von dem Gesicht in das Tuch wischen wollte.*) Itzt wird sie vom Gesichte weg seyn. (*Er nimmt das Schnupftuch an vier Ecken, als ob er etwas darinn Verborgenes tragen wollte, und steht auf.*) Die Ohrfeige trage ich geraden Wegs meinem Herrn nach Hause; er ist ohnehin falsch mit mir umgegangen, und ich hab seinetwegen die Maulschelle unschuldiger Weise bekommen, folgsam gehört sie ihm zu, und nicht mir. (*Will in seines Herrn Haus gehen.*)

Fünfter Auftritt
(*Valere aus dem Hause, und Hans Wurst*).
VAL. (*zu* HW.): Wo willst du hin?

52

HW. (*zornig*): Zu Ihnen in das Haus hab ich gehen wollen.

VAL.: Ist der Brief übergeben? Wo ist die Antwort?

HW.: Den Brief habe ich der Lisette selbst gegeben, und die Antwort ist hier im Schnupftuche.

VAL.: Du Narr! Was soll die Antwort im Schnupftuche?

HW.: Sie wär mir sonst so schwer geworden.

VAL.: Lass sehen! (*reisst dem Hw. das Tuch weg, hält es mit einer Hand, und sieht hinein.*) Wo ist sie denn? Ich seh ja nichts.

HW.: Eben fliegt sie heraus. (*Stosst dem Valere das Tuch ins Gesicht*).

VAL. (*zieht den Degen*): Was? Du verfluchter Hund, das soll dich dein Leben kosten! . . .[34]

No longer the sentimental suicide, as was Leander, Valer is determined not to be thwarted in his plans by either Hasenkopf or Alkantor, and it is largely as a result of this new-found determination on the hero's part, that the final revelation that he has being wooing his sister, has such a profound effect upon him. Nobly he struggles to reconcile himself with Henriette's re-appraisal of the situation:

Die heute so unverhofft entstandene Begebenheit macht, dass ich meiner Schwester zu Liebe die Abreise zum Regimente bis übermorgen verschieben werde. . .[35]

The popular comedian, Hans Wurst, is also better integrated into the course of the plot. His revenge on Jacques, the barber, serves not only the ends of farce, but also provides material for the further development of the plot. The barber gloats in what he thinks is a soliloquy on his financial success in the business of passing information and accounts for each coin of his ill-gotten gains as he drops them into what he thinks is his own hat, but which in effect belongs to Hans Wurst. Hans Wurst then proceeds to give the barber something of his own medicine:

HW. (*als ob er in Gedanken wär*): Das sind zusammen fünf Ducaten, zwey davon gehören noch auf heute, die geb ich meinem betrogenen Herrn wieder zurück. (*Steckt sie in dem Sack.*) Einen Ducaten, den versauf ich für meine Bemühung. (*Steckt ihn ein.*) Ein Ducaten gehört für einige Schab Stroh und zwey spanische Röhre. (*Wie oben.*) Und ein Ducaten gehört zum Trinkgelde für zwey Korporalen, die dem Herrn Friseur Arm und Bein entzwey schlagen. So bleibt die Austheilung, und so sind die fünf Ducaten weg. (*Zum Friseur*). Hab ich Dich erwischt, Du Hausbestie von einem Friseur—so unterstehst Du dich mit ehrlichen Leuten zu verfahren? So betrügst Du meinen gnädigen Herrn, der Dir noch so vieles schenkt?

FRIS. (*voll Angst*): Sie erlauben, Herr Fourierschütz! Sie sind einer irrigen Meinung—die Sache ist ganz anders.

HW.: Was anders? Glaubst Du verdammter Strick, dass ich nicht der ganzen Sache zugehört habe, was meines Herrn Papa, mit Dir geredet hat? Aber Du sollst sehen, mit wem Du zu thun hast. Bring deine peruckenmacherische Seel in Ordnung, Du musst sterben. (*Zieht den Säbel.*)[36]

The popular comedian's almost traditional rôle as an *ungeschickter Sittenlehrer* (clumsy moral tutor) to the hero recurs in this play, when he advises Valer in his love affair. It is the same function which Fuchsmundi fulfilled in 1711 in Stranitzky's *Ollapatrida*,[37] only there is in Hafner's Hans Wurst a far closer association with the *Stadtleben* of Vienna. Like Fuchsmundi he humorously upbraids his master for his sentimentality:

Was wird denn auch so Wichtiges darinn enthalten seyn, als der Verliebten Gewöhnliches: mein Engel!—Ich schmachte;—meine Schöne!—mein Leben!—meine Gebietherinn!—ich küsse Sie in Gedanken;—mein Abgott!—schenken Sie mir Ihr Herz!—ich schwöre Ihnen ewige Treue;—ich sterbe; hohl mich der Teufel! —und dergleichen verliebte Possen. Und es ist doch alles umsonst. . .[38]

Two other characters of the play, although on the surface their rôles are only minor ones, deserve special mention here. The first of these is the *Hausmeister*, or house-steward, a lively expression of Viennese local colour and, as Sonnleithner remarks, an innovation on the Viennese stage. The editor, without any hesitation or modification, gives full credit to Hafner for his originality and for the success and effectiveness of his character-drawing. He continues by equating Hafner's name in this field with Molière, Plautus and Holberg and explains for those unfamiliar with the duties of the house-steward in Vienna, the nature of his employment:

. . . Ich sag' es ohne Bedenken, weder Plautus, noch Molière, noch Holberg haben irgend einen komischen Charakter wahrer aufgefasst, und lebendiger dargestellt. Der Hausmeister ist in Wien in jedem grössern Hause zu finden; er hat gewöhnlich das Maurerhandwerk gelernt. Er wohnt meist auf der Flur; er besorgt die Beleuchtung der Treppen, er weisst die Wände, er besorgt alle kleineren Hausgeschäfte, er bestellt die Aufträge des Hausherrn an die Miethparteien. Alle diese kleineren Geschäfte machen, dass er mit den Verhältnissen der Personen, die ein Haus bewohnen mehr oder weniger bekannt ist, und wer zu einer Stunde, in welcher das Haus geschlossen ist, hinein oder heraus wollte oder etwas in Geheim in das Haus zu bestellen hätte, müsste sich auf irgend eine Weise mit dem Hausmeister abfinden.[39]

Thus by his mere position in the household, the house-steward was already admirably suited for transference into the traditional intrigue which Hafner inherited from the *commedia dell' arte*. Caricature in this case is transcended by Hafner, for the house-steward is not a type—although quite naturally his employment demands some stylization—but a character. This is shown by the implantation of individual features over and above those which are proper to the man's occupation. For instance, the steward is hard of hearing, which might well be the case, pretended or not, amongst Viennese stewards in general. Hafner's character, however, is not content with this and where he hears nothing, he humorously creates in his own words what he believes he has missed:

VAL.: Ich weiss nicht, was ich mit dem Rindvieh anfangen soll. (*Zum Hausm.*) Hört, guter Freund! Schläft Henriette noch?

HAUSM.: Ey freylich. Sie wird sich erst niedergelegt haben; denn sie und ich haben die ganze Nacht kein Maul zugemacht.

VAL.: Und warum denn nicht?

HAUSM.: Wie? Was sagen Sie?

VAL.: Warum seyd Ihr denn immer munter gewesen?

HAUSM.: Ja, es ist gewiss wahr.

HW. (*schreyt überlaut*): Warum er nichts geschlafen hat, fragt mein gnädiger Herr! (*Vor sich.*) Der Kerl muss eine Doppelthür vor den Ohren haben.

HAUSM.: Ich versteh es schon. Wir haben nicht schlafen dürfen, denn unser alter Herr fürchtet sich vor den Geistern erschrecklich, und da kommen sie öfters bey der Nacht, und discuriren mit ihm; und heut Nacht hätte die Trud auch wieder kommen sollen, drum haben wir die ganze Nacht beym ihm wachen müssen, das Fräulein und ich; ich hab auf die Geister Acht haben müssen, und das Fräulein auf die Trud.

VAL. (*vor sich*): Was gibt es doch für Thoren in der Welt! (*Zum Hausm.*) Aber itzt könnt Ihr ja sehr leicht dem Fräulein den Brief bringen.

HAUSM.: Ja, ja, die Trud kömmt öfters zu meinem Herrn, und da steigt sie auf ihn hinauf, und saugt drey Seitel oder gar ein Mass Blut, darnach sie durstig ist, und nachdem geht sie wieder fort, und mein Herr wird entsetzlich krank darauf.

VAL.: Hier ist der Brief, itzt frag ich Euch zum letzten Mahl, wollt Ihr ihn überbringen oder nicht?

HAUSM.: Nein, nein, ich kann nicht, ich darf nicht, ich will nicht, ich trau mir nicht, ich soll nicht, ich mag nicht.

VAL. (*zum Hausm.*): So will ich Euch denn sagen——

HAUSM. (*zornig*): Was schlagen? Mich schlagen? Ihr Brod ist nicht in meinem Dienst. Itzt geh ich gleich, und sag es meinem Herrn—Sie sollen mir Schläg antragen? (*Eine Weile stillstehend, auf ein Mahl wieder zornig.*) Was? Wie? Wer ist ein Flegel? Ich bin kein Kuppler? Ich bin ein ehrlicher Kerl—mein Herr wird Ihnen schon weisen, was zu weisen ist. (*Lauft zornig in das Haus ab.*)[40]

His part is also quite well integrated into the intrigue. His drunken monologue in Act III sc. iv., which provides comedy relevant to the plot, motivates the sleep which finally overpowers him in Act III, sc. x and renders him appropriately oblivious to events in the final scene. There is a new subtlety also introduced in the characterization of Alkantor, whose villainous intent in the intrigue has been to prevent a union between Valer and Henriette. In the finale he is revealed as a good person, who has all the time been working on the side of good, seeking to avoid a catastrophe. His evidence, produced in the final scene, that the hero and heroine are in fact brother and sister, brings to light the deceit on which the action of the play was founded.

The plot of Hafner's *Etwas zum Lachen im Fasching*[41] in its essential features is again the same which forms the basis of his other plays. Now, however, the main emphasis has shifted somewhat. The traditional hero of the original plot of the *commedia dell'arte* has no part in this play, and it is taken over by a popular figure, Burlin—the creation of Anton Brenner—who becomes the play's leading character. The intrigue reflects, therefore, some influence also from the Don Juan and Doktor Faustus tradition of the Viennese popular theatre, presented earlier in Stranitzky's

Leben und todt Doctor Faustus and *Das steinerne Gastmahl,*
continued by Karl Marinelli in his *Don Juan oder: Der steinerne Gast,* which was performed several times in Vienna from
its première in 1783 until 1821,[42] and by Schikaneder in his four-
act allegoric play *Schembera, Herr von Boskowitz* (1808).[43]

Burlin, originally conceived as a *Volksnarr,* is not the usual
extrovert, popular comedian, although in the traditional manner
he is subjected to the parody of suicide. He has a genial nature,
but is potentially a tragic figure, a facet of his character which
is clearly presented early in the play:

> ... Nero hat seine Mutter mit einem Dolch ermordet, du aber,
> Bösewicht, wirst deinen Vater zu Tod tanzen. (*Er weint und
> fängt gleich wieder zu lachen an.*) Aber einen walzerischen habens
> aufgemacht, auf den will ich mein Lebtag denken. Das deutsche
> Tanzen ist halt doch weit lustiger als der Menuet. (*Er fängt an
> einen walzerischen zu geigen, und springt und tanzt rechtschaffen
> herum.*[44]

Almost an uncontrollable schizophrenic, Burlin's effectiveness
is twofold. On the one hand sympathy for him is roused, as he
never indulges in self-pity despite an incredibly long series of
catastrophes. These all begin after he has acquired 250 ducats in
Act II, sc. vi. In Act II, sc. viii the solicitor and guards relieve
him of his clothes and his money, in sc. x of the same act, after
he has been given some clothes by Pantalon, he is stripped by
the caterer and guards, in sc. xii he is robbed by two barons and
in Act III, sc. i a Jew robs him of jewellery worth 11,000 Fl. Yet
in many respects Burlin is completely insensitive to other people
and he deals with the two girls who are in love with him—
Nanette and Rosalia—in a completely heartless manner, regarding their immediate and hereditary fortunes as their only attraction. His failing, which has the implications of a social disease
of Viennese nouveau-riche society, particularly at Carnival
time (Sonnleithner remarks in a footnote that he once knew a
person who sold his bed on the Monday so that he could go to
the masked ball on the Tuesday), is his inability to practise
economy. He is powerless to contain the urge for ostentatious
display, and yet he shows a sincere awareness of his guilt. There
is no development of his character and he is aware of his failings
to the same degree at the beginning of the play as at the end.
Only at the end, however, is it absolutely clear that he is incor-

rigible, despite his penitent promise to do service as a musketeer and an attempt to blame his financial degradation on the Carnival. Hans Wurst plays his traditional rôle as servant to the leading male character and confidant in moral and amatory matters, and the solicitor is further evidence of Hafner's talent as a portrayer of character. As in the case of the house-steward in *Der Furchtsame,* he receives individual treatment beyond the stylizing power of his occupation, when he allows his personal feelings to hinder him in what should be the rigorous performance of his professional duties. His fleeting moment of sympathy with the plight of Burlin and Hans Wurst is, however, his downfall, and he is finally deserted by them, as he stands alone, now with no sympathy for them, and no clothes.[45]

Hafner's *Die bürgerliche Dame*[46] appears to have been a variation on a theme by Molière, but the situation of the intrigue is clearly that of the author's other plays and of the plot he inherited from the *commedia dell'arte.* Like the latter two plays it is essentially a comedy of character with the main character this time a society-conscious female. In the course of the plot, Frau Redlichinn (whose husband is very aptly named), now that her husband has been absent for two years, parades herself, her daughter and her household, as paragons of the upper crust, ignoring in the meantime the limitations which her husband's bourgeois finances impose. Whilst suffering a similar degradation to Burlin, it is felt that the lady is merely letting down her hair, whereas Burlin's complete disregard of the need to practise economy was inborn. The suspicion that Frau Redlichinn is mentally sick, founded on her insane protestations of innocence, even when her guilt is obvious to everyone towards the end of the play, excites some unusual sympathy for her predicament and, of course, tends to diminish her moral responsibility. Persistent reference is made to her previously unimpeachable behaviour and it is clearly inferred that her husband's prolonged absence is the cause of her various misdemeanours. The intensity of her belief in the almost divine right of her aristocratic status, condemns her as a person who is seeking to exceed the bounds of her natural, accorded position in life.

Like Burlin she is potentially a tragic figure as she continues to strive for an ideal, which she herself recognizes, but dare not acknowledge as unattainable. Nevertheless sympathy for her plight is roused, as she senses that she is caught up in the vortex which inevitably leads to absolute corruption. Frau Redlichinn—again like Burlin—is penitent but helpless, the affection she showers on her daughter revealing her mental anguish. In a soliloquy, which is remarkable on the popular stage, for its psychological insight, Frau Redlichinn reveals the duality of impulses which have motivated her actions. As a woman who has been emotionally overwrought, she gradually overcomes her piqued senses by reason, and subsequently humbles herself as a true penitent:

> Rache, Scham, Reue und Furcht bemeistern sich meiner Seele—ich bin von allen Seiten hintergangen und beschimpft! Was wird die Welt—was werden die Bekannten von mir sagen? Doch was hat die Welt und Bekannten vormahls von mir sagen können? In was unglückseligen Umständen befindest du dich, ärmste Redlichinn!—aber hattest du dir wohl ein andres End deiner Ausschweifungen vermuthen können? Alles geht verlohren!—die Hochachtung, die man gegen mich-doch wer hatte sie gegen mich bezeugt, ausser Leuten, die ich, mir solche zu bezeugen, zu meinem Schaden beschenkt habe?[47]

To assess the influence of one playwright on another in an age where plagiarism, subconscious or otherwise, was part of the contemporary tradition, is a difficult matter, as is the establishment of the association beween Hafner and Schikaneder. Almost without doubt, the two playwrights never met, for when Hafner died in 1764 Schikaneder was only 13 years old, and in any case, according to his sole biographer, Egon Komorzynski, did not come to Vienna until 1784. But with reference to products, instead of to personalities, some mutual association can be supposed. The programme of theatre performances by Schikaneder's company in Salzburg in 1780 was copied and sent by Maria Anna Thekla Mozart to Wolfgang on November 30 and December 18 of that year. In the list, she entered for October: "den 26ten die 42te comedie. burlins faschings begebenheiten, diese farce hast du schon beym böhm gesehen",[48] clearly the above mentioned play *Etwas zum Lachen im Fasching*. Of course, this is only one known instance of Schikaneder's first-hand acquaintance with Hafner's plays, but the widespread success, which Rommel declares was the lot of *Megära*,[49] and Hafner's fame as the "Vater des Weiner Volksstücks", would indicate that Schikaneder could not have been in ignorance of Hafner's plays in general.

In Vienna in 1786 Wenzel Müller and Karl Hensler joined Marinelli's Leopoldstadttheater, a rival theatre to Schikaneder's Freihaustheater, as Master of Music and Composer, and Theatre-Poet respectively. Together with another writer for the theatre, Joachim Perinet, Müller produced a long series of extremely successful, popular *Singspiele* in the last decade of the century, many of them adaptations from Hafner.[50] From 1798 to 1803 Perinet was a member of Schikaneder's theatre, and when the adventurous impresario moved to his newly built Theater an der Wien in 1801, Perinet's name appeared in the dramatis personae of an occasional play *Thespis* by Schikaneder, which was the last play performed in the Freihaustheater and which advertised to the audience the new theatre which was to be opened on the following day. In the play Perinet played the part of Angelaus. Later in 1803 Perinet edited the Viennese Theatre Almanac of that year and had only praise for Schikaneder's work. His two poetic discourses on Mozart and Schikaneder: *Mozart und Schikaneder. Ein theatralisches Gespräch über die Aufführung der Zauberflöte im Stadttheater* (1801) (*A theatrical Discourse about the Performance of the Magic Flute in the City Theatre*) and *Ein theatralisches Gespräch zwischen Mozart und Schikaneder über den Verkauf des Theaters* (1802) (*Theatrical Discourse between Mozart and Schikaneder on the Sale of the Theatre*) give evidence of quite a close relationship with, and understanding of, Schikaneder, and it must be near the truth to suppose, that Perinet in some way acted as a middle-man between Hafner's works and Schikaneder where the latter did not already know of them. The editor of Hafner's collected works, Joseph Sonnleithner, acknowledges Schikaneder's indebtedness to Hafner, and his advance beyond Hafner, in the genre known as *Lokalstück*.[51]

4

THE GROWTH OF *SINGSPIEL* IN SOUTHERN GERMANY

By the end of the century the *Singspiel* form had gained an astonishing degree of popularity in the Vienna of Haydn and Mozart, and undoubtedly the expression of its highest excellence, musically speaking, was the latter's final work for the stage, *The Magic Flute*, first performed in Schikaneder's Freihaustheater on September 30, 1791. Its appearance, however, was not that of a single star in a darkened sky, as Miss Brophy's recent book *Mozart the Dramatist*[1] has presupposed, but of one star in a constellation of many. *The Magic Flute* outshone the others of course, but the way to its creation was prepared by a profusion of earlier *Singspiele*, which established the genre on the South German stage in general, and on the Viennese suburban stages in particular.

The Old Viennese Popular Theatre played an important part in the growth of *Singspiel*. It was not responsible for the original creation of the form of the genre, for many of the foreign influences on the *Volksstück* of the theatre were previously familiar with the form of dialogue interspersed with song, but the theatre did succeed in channelling both external and internal forces into one main stream, which fed the Viennese *Volksstück* essentially and the *Singspiel* incidentally. In the previous century the so-called *Englische* or *Niederländische Comödianten* had introduced to the Continent what in all probability was the forerunner of the German *Singspiel*, the *singetspiel*, which consisted of verse set to music.[2] From a comparison between the text of one of their works, *Pickelhering in der Kiste* (1620),[3] translated from the English *Singing Simpkin*, and of a later *Singspiel*, *Der Dorfbarbier* (1770), by Johann Adam Hiller and Christian Felix Weisse (one of the most successful partnerships of the strolling stage in Schikaneder's day),[4] it would appear that although the two works are separated by 150 years, both styles of popular theatre, that

61

of the *Englische Comödianten* and that of the strolling stage in Germany, had much in common. However, it is difficult to go further in assessing the influence of the first on the one contemporary with Schikaneder. A definite influence on the Old Viennese Popular Theatre was, of course, the *commedia dell' arte*, but this only became noticeable after the death of Joseph Anton Stranitzky in 1727. Then, in the time of Gottfried Prehauser, when several Italian as well as German actors and comedians came to the theatre, and later in the 1760's in the works of Hafner, there was some considerable manifestation of the Italian influence. The part of the *commedia* in the growth of music in the Viennese popular theatre has, however, not been noted. A further influence on the popular stage made itself felt in Paris, and this was via the *Singspiele* of Evariste Gherardi's Théâtre Italien, which, in Vienna, reflected the influence of the Parisian *théâtres de la foire* of the late seventeenth century. It has been noted by Rommel that the vaudevilles of the *théâtres de la foire* were themselves forerunners of the *opéra comique*, which was developed in the middle of the eighteenth century by E. R. Duni and C. W. Gluck and which in turn influenced the *Singspiele* of Weisse and Hiller. An additional Italian influence on the *Singspiel* in Vienna was caused by the arrival in the first half of the century, of light, burlesque operettas, or *Kurzopern*, from Venice, Naples and Rome, when the Imperial Court saw fit to exercise some control over the repertoire of the popular theatre. The two Italian impresarios, Borosini and Selliers, who had assumed management of the Kärntnerthortheater after the death of Stranitzky in 1727, soon expressed to the Court a desire to further the cause of Italian opera, but they suffered a temporary setback on discovering that the Court had already granted a Royal Licence for Opera, albeit unused, to one Francesco Bellini. A compromise was reached, when the Imperial Court, neither wishing to abuse Bellini's privilege on the one hand, nor wishing on the other to bar the impresario's path to the operettas, decreed that the Italians might only produce the said operettas, alongside the German plays, which were already being performed there. The decree had effect from 1728 until 1741 and thus imposed on the popular stage a genre of similar construction to the *opéra comique*, prose dialogue, that is, the German comedies, with musical insertions, that is, the Italian *Kurzopern*.[5]

62

Increasing interest in music and *Singspiel* manifested itself also in the activities of individual members of the popular theatre. Stranitzky was certainly not renowned for his musical ability, but his successor, Gottfried Prehauser, over and above his versatility as actor, improvisor, and comedian, possessed a good singing voice. As Stranitzky had done before him, when he had adapted the libretti of Italian Grand Opera and of the baroque theatre in Vienna, reducing the musical appeal as he did so, to the form of his *Haupt- und Staatsaktionen*, so now did Prehauser continue in the same vein, adapting the plots of serious drama and opera to suit the demands of popular taste, specifically, according to Richard Smekal, to include "comic accessories".[6] Assisted by Prehauser's greater versatility in comedy and by his musical ability, these accessories developed in an independent state to form the genre which came to be known as *komisches Singspiel*. This internal development and growth of the *Singspiel* form coincided, of course, with the external pressures from the Imperial Court and the Italian management, and the foreign influences from Italy and France.

A comedian contemporary with Prehauser, Joseph Kurz, who won local fame as the creator of the popular figure known as Bernardon, together with his Italian-born wife, Franziska, an excellent soprano singer, gave further impetus to the development of *Singspiel*. Like Prehauser, Kurz had musical talent, so much so that in one play he could sing the parts of Pharmaces, Cosroe, and Ormechus, treble, tenor, and bass, respectively.[7] The *Teutsche Arien*, which were in the repertory of the popular theatre from 1737 to 1757, bore witness to the increasing musical interest of the theatre and its audience, and were clearly intended to be presented on stage in the manner of intermezzi. The love of music shared by Kurz and his wife—it is reported by Robert Haas that the latter was pleased to accept serenades from young, admiring musicians—led to an association with Joseph Haydn, which resulted in the production of one of the first known *Singspiele* of the era, *Der neue krumme Teufel* (1752). Haas relates the humorous encounter between Kurz and Haydn:

> . . . Beide Personen fanden sich, Haydn musste dem Kurz in die Wohnung folgen. "Setzen Sie sich zum Flügel und begleiten Sie die Pantomime, die ich Ihnen vormachen werde, mit einer passen-

den Musik. Stellen Sie sich vor, Bernardon sei ins Wasser gefallen und suchte sich durch Schwimmen zu retten". Nun ruft er seinen Bedienten, wirft sich mit dem Bauch quer über einen Sessel, lässt den Stuhl von dem Bedienten im Zimmer hin und herziehen und bewegt sich, während Haydn im Sechsachteltakt das Spiel der Wellen und das Schwimmen ausdrückt, mit Armen und Beinen wie ein Schwimmender. Plötzlich springt Bernardon auf, umarmt Haydn und erstickt ihn beinahe mit Küssen. "Haydn, Sie sind ein Mann für mich! Sie müssen mir eine Oper schreiben!" So entstand der krumme Teufel, Haydn erhielt 25 Dukaten dafür und hielt sich für sehr reich. Diese Oper wurde mit grossem Beifall zweimal aufgeführt und darauf wegen beleidigender Anzüglichkeiten im Text verboten.[8]

Although this was the work of two Austrians, the majority of the associations of the *Singspiel* were Italian. In the first place it was allegedly a satire at the expense of the Italian impresario Afflisio, who had succeeded Borosini and Selliers, and was subsequently banned after two or three performances; its intermezzo was a short scene in the manner of the *commedia dell' arte* and was written in Italian; the décor, in the tradition of the Old Viennese Popular Theatre, remained true to the lavish baroque settings and "power-scenes" of the Italian Court Opera. The native element of the *Singspiel* might, however, be discernible in so far as it represented a parody of such theatrical effusion. Kurz's own words at the end of the text, suggest a further influence from France, for he himself does not assess its genre as *Singspiel*, but as *opéra comique*.[9]

Two years after Hafner's death in 1764, there appeared in print a magic *Singspiel* with the title *Lisuart und Dariolette*, which was to be produced in the following year on the stage of the Old Viennese Popular Theatre, from which it was to travel widely on the German strolling stage, until in 1777 in Nuremberg, Schikaneder became intimately acquainted with it, himself playing the title rôle of Lisuart. During his time on the strolling stage the operetta was performed on several occasions by Schikaneder's company.[10] The libretto of the *Singspiel* was written by Daniel Scheibeler and the music composed by Johann Adam Hiller. It appears that its reception in Vienna was quite favourable, and certainly it enjoyed great popularity on the strolling stage in the 1770's and provided Schikaneder with one

Tamino, design by Joseph Hoffmann.

Sarastro, design by Joseph Hoffmann.

of the forerunners to a spate of magic operas, which were to be performed in his two Viennese theatres after 1789, and to a quantity of the same genre which were to be produced some little time later by Hensler and Perinet in Marinelli's Leopoldstadt-theater. The dramatis personae include a reference to English legend where the Queen appears as "Ginevra, King Arthur's widow", and Schiebeler in fact acknowledges an English source, Chaucer's "Tale of the Wife of Bath", as translated into "modern" English in a collection of Dryden's fables, the same source, comments Schiebeler, as Voltaire's *Ce qui plaît aux dames*.

The Beggar's Opera, by John Gay and Dr. Pepusch, which had its première in London on January 29, 1728, was an unprecedented success. One of its sucessors in England, however, *The Devil to Pay* by C. Coffey and J. Mottley, had a more direct influence on the growth of *Singspiel* in Germany, when it appeared in Berlin in 1731. It was performed by the Schönemann company in the German translation by K. W. Borcke, with the original music, to which its failure there has been attributed. The work was produced in two parts: *The Wives Metamorphosed* and *The Merry Cobler*. Weisse's adaptations of the same *Singspiel*, *Die verwandelten Weiber oder der Teufel ist los* and *Der lustige Schuster oder der zweyte Theil vom Teufel ist los*, which with new music by Standfuss, were performed in Leipzig by G. H. Koch's company, met with only limited success. Only later in 1766 and 1768 respectively, when Hiller set both parts to music, did they become popular.[11] This was at the same time as the first appearance of *Lisuart und Dariolette*, but it appears from Schiebeler's title-page and references, if not from the actual genre of magic *Singspiel*, that the work did not spring directly from the tradition of *The Beggar's Opera*. In the time of Prehauser, music and magic had been earlier introduced into the repertoire of the Old Viennese Popular Theatre, as it struggled for survival against the infiltration of literary drama and sought to attract its audience into the theatre by means of such external accessories. *Lisuart und Dariolette*, despite an English source, has more in common with a specifically Viennese tradition.

Hiller was very much influenced by the French *opéra comique* and his association with Weisse in the production of *Singspiele* for the German strolling stage revealed what was then an uncommon virtue by acknowledging sources. In Hiller's case these were mostly French, occasionally English. None of the Hiller *Singspiele*, popular as they were, originating in Leipzig, touching on Vienna and comparatively storming the strolling stage, can be described textually as German in conception. Schiebeler's English source for *Lisuart und Dariolette* was Chaucer, Weisse's text *Der Teufel ist los* acknowledged Charles Coffey, his *Lottchen am Hofe* acknowledged Favart's *Le caprice amoureux* or *Ninette à la cour*; *Der Dorfbarbier* was indebted to F. Philidor's and M. Sedaine's *Blaise le Savetier* of 1759, and *Die Jagd* to a French historical comedy *La partie de chasse de Henri IV* by C. Collé. The sources for his *Die Liebe auf dem Lande* were given as Favart's *Annette à Lubin* and Aseaume's *La Clochette*. Even the *Singspiel* of Mozart, *Bastien et Bastienne* (1768), was in the same line of French inheritance, its text being the German version by F. W. Weiskern, a leading comedian of the Old Viennese Popular Theatre under Prehauser, of Favart's parody of Rousseau's *Le devin du village*.[12]

As all known *Singspiele* prior to 1775 seem to betray their origins or predominant influence from abroad, it has become a matter of some interest to discover the first truly German *Singspiel*, textually speaking. Hitherto it has been assumed that the honours for this were borne off by Paul Weidmann in 1778, the year in which Joseph II instituted the *Teutsches Nationalsingspiel* in Vienna as an adjunct to the *Hof- und Nationaltheater*, which he had founded earlier with the same patriotic intent. Certainly Weidmann appears to have obeyed the Emperor's wishes in that matter, for his *Die Bergknappen* (1778) with music by I. Umlauf: "an original *Singspiel* in one act", can boast distinctly German rather than foreign origins. Unfortunately for Weidmann the work appeared two years too late and he was thus robbed of a little fame by that later much maligned librettist, Emanuel Schikaneder, whose thoroughly German, most probably autobiographical, *Singspiel* of *De Lyranten oder das lustige Elend* was published in Innsbruck in 1776, having been performed, according to the author's note, on several occasions before that date:

Da das Publikum diesen ersten Versuch eines der Schaubühne gewidmeten Liebhabers der Musen mit einigem Beyfalle aufgenommen hat, so hat sich derselbe überreden lassen, dieses Stück nach vorgenommenen merklichen Verbesserungen in den Druck zu geben. Liebhaber der Musik und des Theaters, die Geschmack haben, werden ihm nach dem Grade des Beyfalls Aufmunterung oder Stillschweigen zuwinken.[13]

An earlier comedy by Weidmann, *Der Bettelstudent oder das Donnerwetter* (1776), was a free adaptation from the Spanish *Die Höhle von Cuenço* by Cervantes,[14] and its genre is in fact not far removed from that of *Singspiel*. Yet the only songs in the work, and these are very sparse in number—sparser even than in the comedies of Hafner, whose works likewise never received the title of *Singspiel*—involve only the main character, the student Wilhelm. Nor is there any chorus involvement, as there was previously in Hiller, and in 1776 in Schikaneder's *Die Lyranten*. The comedy with musical insertions, if such it may be called, was, nevertheless, a success.

Of the known *Singspiele* of the new era Schikaneder's *Die Lyranten* was unique. Its overwhelming success on the strolling stage is all the more astounding, as Schikaneder first began his stage career in 1773, when he registered in the company of Andreas Schopf at the age of 22. By 1775 he was already earning some success as producer and singer with the same company in Innsbruck,[15] and it was probably during this time that *Die Lyranten* was first performed. It is not known whether Schikaneder was previously acquainted with the *Singspiel* form, but it would be hard to believe that he wasn't. To Schikaneder's further credit he wrote not only the libretto but also the music to *Die Lyranten,* and accordingly the Gotha *Theaterkalender* of 1777 and 1778 list him as *Tonkünstler*. From the text it would seem that Schikaneder was at least one step ahead of Weisse, who published his views on *Singspiel* in the preface to an edition of his libretti in 1777.[16] By 1775 Schikaneder had already advanced beyond Weisse's rather restrictive recommendations, which advised the depiction of naïve rusticity, of pastoral happiness, and the song's representation of "one simple emotion". With regard to the latter, it is, however, to be noted that in *Die Lyranten* the *Stimmungslied* ("song of mood") which may be said to present "one simple emotion", predominated over the *Rollenlied* ("song of role") which had previously characterized the majority of songs in the *Teutsche Arien* and the repertoire of the Old Viennese Popular Theatre. But Schikaneder was ignorant of Weisse's advice, unless he had learnt something from his theatrical works, and he also appears to have been ignorant of Wieland's exhortation to the librettists of *Singspiel* to turn for their subject matter to "the age of wandering knights" and the "bucolic world of the poets",[17] for his *Die Lyranten* is remarkable, not only amongst contemporary *Singspiele*, but also amongst his other theatrical works, in that it reveals no visible indebtedness to any other theatrical tradition, foreign or native, apart from of course the popular stage in general terms. No predecessor to *Die Lyranten* has yet been discovered prior to 1775 which is as purely German in its text. Perhaps the real secret of its success, of the vitality of its text compared with the pastoral insipidity of Weisse and the comic trickery of the Old Viennese Popular Theatre, is to be found, as Komorzynski has suggested, in the fact that in writing it Schikaneder drew from his personal experiences as a wandering musician of the German stage. Schikaneder has been widely criticized, not without some irrelevancy, for his enthusiasm for the presentation of spectacle on stage, but even his most prejudiced critic would have to concede that *Die Lyranten*, admittedly unlike any other of his works in some respects, contains no such element, but stands by its idea, its text, and—so far as may be judged—its music which is no longer extant.

Musically it would appear that Schikaneder's work offered greater complexity than that of Hiller, although it is still to be presumed that his music was "popular". Only individual instances of song can be described in Weisse's terms as "das kleine gesellschaftliche Lied". Act I contains 6 arias, 1 allegro, 1 march off, 1 duet and 1 chorus, Act II has 8 arias and 1 allegro, and Act III, 1 recitative and aria, 1 aria and allegro and the final chorus. Within the one *Singspiel* Schikaneder provides songs which obey Weisse's maxim in making their appeal by way of a simple, catchy melody, and those which are effective by their rhythmic impact. Stock's aria, "Ein Weibsbild ist ein närrisch Ding" ("A woman is a foolish creature") is a song of little textual import, and its fame in Germany and Vienna can only be attributed to the melody of the first line—textually and musically—which, unadulterated, comprises eight of the sixteen lines. In contrast to this song, Schikaneder's use of recitative in Act I is seen as an integral part of dramatic function, where the tempo of a theatrical situation is manifest in the rhythmic quality of

the text and requires little melodic embellishment to fulfil its
purpose:

WIRTHINN:
Wisset, ihr zerlumpte Schrollen!
Dass ich Frau vom Hause bin?
Ihr sollt euch von hinnen trollen!

ALLE:
Frau, das gehet nicht so hin:
Wir sind Gäste, die bezahlen.

SCHULMEISTER:
Ich Schulmeister will vor allen
Viel mehr Respekt, viel mehr Respekt!
Denn ich bin ein gelehrter Mann.

WIRTHINN:
Der immer in dem Wirthaus steckt,
Mit Lumpen zecht, und saufen kann.
Fort, fort aus meinem Haus!

SCHULMEISTER:
Ich bin Schulmeister.

WIRTHINN:
Fort fort hinaus!

BAUER:
Ich bin Geschworner.

WIRTHINN:
Fort fort hinaus!

LEICHTSINN:
Ich bin gereister—

WIRTHINN:
Fort fort hinaus!

STOCK:
Ich ein gebohrner—

WIRTHINN:
Fort fort hinaus!

LEICHTSINN:
Violinist!

STOCK:
Bassist!

WIRTHINN:
Hinaus mit dem Mist!...[18]

69

Generally the transition from dialogue to song proceeds quite smoothly in *Die Lyranten,* the musical nature of the profession of the three leading male characters itself justifying any such interruption in the continuity. Thus it is quite natural in Act I, sc. iv, for Rosina, the heroine, to ask Vogel, the hero and one of the three wandering musicians, to join her in a song, for, she says, she has heard that students such as he sing very well indeed. In at least one instance Schikaneder heightens the tone of the dialogue immediately preceding the song, so that the latter arises naturally from the general atmosphere. In Act II, sc. vii, the proprietress of the village inn and one of the musicians, Leichtsinn, become enamoured of each other, so much so that the former bursts into song praising the looks of the latter:

WIRTHINN: Mein Herr! ich hätte Sie gern etwas verdienen lassen: Sie wissen ohne das, die Leute sind zu wunderlich; sie rechnen alles zum Uebeln aus. Und der Schulmeister, der hat immer das grösste Getümmel. Auf den Abend, dann kann man schon eher eine Lustbarkeit gestatten, als mitten im Tage: ich halte selbst gern mit, und es wird mich freuen Sie noch besser kennen zu lernen.

LEICHTSINN (*küsst ihr die Hand*): Sie sind allzugütig Frau Wirthinn, und Ihre himmelblauen Augen, hol mich der Plunder! wenn sie mich nicht verführen!

WIRTHINN: Und Ihre schwarzen sind eben so gefährlich.

ARIE

Man müsste fühllos und von Stein,
Und nicht ein Frauenzimmer seyn!
Ein holdes schwarzes Aug zu sehn,
Worunter so ein Angesicht
Von Freundlichkeit und Wonne spricht;
Und nicht in Flammen zu vergehn!

2

Wem dieser hönigsüsse Blick
Das Herze nicht entzücken sollte;
Wer hier noch streng, noch melancholisch bleiben wollte:
Verdiente nie ein zärtlich Glück.
O nein! o nein! ich will kein Stein,
Ich will ein Frauenzimmer seyn.[19]

In *Die Lyranten* the *Singspiel* can no longer be regarded in its former, awkward purity, as dialogue form with musical insertions, as the fusion of the two elements has become at once more natural and more complete.

The function of song in *Die Lyranten* extends beyond Weisse's naïve demands and is used by Schikaneder for a variety of theatrical purposes, such as the portrayal of realism, humour, character, events and for the ends of exposition and dramatic effect. The opening arias and allegro by Leichtsinn and Stock, two of the musicians, contain much of this variety in the one musical episode. As a low-class wandering musician, Liechtsinn displays a humorous incongruity when he adopts the courtly fashion of waxing his hair. For the moment he and Stock surrender to "Amor" but their ideas of what love has to offer, are individual. Leichtsinn sings of the outward beauty of love and its intriguing tenderness, but humorously realizes that the catch is that beautiful ladies demand love in return. Stock is more practical in his approach, and looks forward to the time when he will be married and his wife will mend his trousers, darn his socks, and regard him as her one and only concern in life. Characteristically, his preference is for bread and not lemonade. His vocabulary reflects a French influence on the libretto, but in so doing determines only the characterization, as the work in no way recalls Weisse's adapting of French originals.[20]

Schikaneder is known to have produced another three new *Singspiele* on the strolling stage, all first appearing in 1786, ten years later than *Die Lyranten*. Of one of these, *Das urianische Schloss*,[21] little is known, but neither of the others can boast either the German purity, the uniqueness and vitality, nor even the same degree of success as *Die Lyranten*. The first of these *Der Luftballon*,[22] of which only the text of the songs remains extant, can be praised for a degree of German flavour in its content. It is distinguished by its popular tone and rather moralizing attitudes, it reflects to a small extent the worship of reason in the contemporary age of enlightenment, and there is a measure of successful characterization as popular terminology and thought are placed in the mouths of the appropriate class, in this case the ship's captain and the proprietress of the inn, and the language of the romanticized heroic couple, Leblanc and Sophie, is likewise appropriately treated. Included in this work, judging from the continuity of the songs, is the idea of moral purification which recurs again in *The Magic Flute*, and indeed Komorzynski has used this as his starting point to show that the two works were written by the same librettist. There is no magic in the plot, but the balloon flight was clearly intended to similarly reduce the audience to a state of wonderment. Its closest parallel is to the probations of fire and water in *The Magic Flute*: Tamino and Pamina undergo them together and emerge not only triumphant, but initiated into the priesthood. In *Der Luftballon*, Leblanc and Sophie suffer the ordeal of a dangerous flight by balloon and ultimately experience, apart from their idealized, mutual love and respect of course, what they term a "harmony of soul". The work was written as an occasional play to celebrate what was to be Baron Lütgendorf's successful flight from Augsburg on August 24, 1786. Due to a technical hitch admitted on September 4, the project was revealed as a hoax, and neither the flight nor Schikaneder's *Singspiel* ever took place.[23] It would be inadvisable to claim that the idea of the textual representation of a balloon flight was an original one of Schikaneder's, as three works for the stage, two of them printed in Augsburg and Munich, all of them appearing in the same year, 1786, suggest by their very presence the partial embodiment of a wider tradition, which followed hard upon the success of the Montgolfier brothers in Paris in 1783. Of these three, *Die Luftbälle oder die Liebhaber à la Montgolfier*, a two-act farce by Brezner, *Die Luftschiffer oder der Strafplanet der Erde*, a three-act *komisch-satirisches Original-Singspiel* by M. Blumhofer, and *Die Luftschiffer*, a three-act comedy, the first would appear from its title, which expresses the same pattern of events as *Der Luftballon*, and from the fact that it appeared in print in Munich, to be the one most closely related to Schikaneder's *Singspiel*. It is not known, however, which of the two came first. Schikaneder's third *Singspiel* of 1786, *Balders Tod*, a heroic *Singspiel* with Germanic legend as its basis, was merely a translation from the Danish by J. Ewald. Nevertheless it has been surmised, somewhat optimistically, that the work heralded the opera of Wagner.[24]

In Vienna Joseph II had been encouraged to institute the *Teutsches Nationalsingspiel* in 1778 by the success of Johannes Böhm's productions of *Singspiel* in Brünn and the latter was subsequently employed to give *Singspiele* in the Kärntnerthor-theater alongside the costly and spectacular ballet given by Noverre. This had afforded Böhm little independence and after two months and five performances of *Singspiel* he had left the theatre. Joseph's project had been handicapped in the first place by lack of material and in the second because the best and most influential singers were Italian, with, of course, their own views on patriotic conscience. Ignaz Umlauf, hitherto a violinist in the orchestra, was appointed director of the *Singspiel* and Umlauf it was who wrote the music to Weidmann's *Die Bergknappen*, the opera which opened the *Singspiel* enterprise on February 18, 1778.[25] J. H. W. Müller was leader of the orchestra and Stephanie and Schmidt wrote several additional *Singspiele* which were favourably received.[26]

The project was unfortunately seriously undermined by the machinations of the Italians, amongst whom Antonio Salieri, composer to the Imperial Viennese Court from 1774, and *Hofkapellmeister* and director of the Viennese Opera from 1788, and his favourite pupil, the leading soprano, Catarina Cavalieri, figured prominently. At their hands Mozart also suffered, particularly with the performances of *Die Entführung* and *Figaro* and the cold reception in Vienna of *Don Giovanni*. Despite both Joseph's and Mozart's patriotic endeavours, the enterprise in Vienna was doomed to failure. As early as December 13, 1782, a comedy with ariettas by Umlauf, entitled *Welche ist die beste Nation?*, received a damning criticism by Mozart in his letters, and a repeat performance was an equal failure.[27] Mozart further criticized *Der Rauchfangkehrer* (1781) by Auenbrugger and Salieri as a wretched work, in doing so acknowledging somewhat reluctantly, that the opera was German and not Italian. As a measure of Mozart's talent against the mediocrity of other German and Italian composers, Anfossi's *Il curioso indiscreto*, performed on June 30, 1783, was an utter failure, apart from two arias, which Mozart had written for Madame Lange. By March 12, 1783, Mozart had expressed extreme doubt as to the continued existence of the German *Singspiel*, as conceived by Joseph.

Aware of the impending failure of the enterprise Joseph sought to provide alternative accommodation for the genre as early as February, 1781, when he granted Marinelli and Menninger permission to build a theatre in the Leopoldstadt. When this was opened on October 20 in the same year, it provided Vienna, at least theoretically, with new hope for the cause of

German theatre and the *Singspiel*, for, in the suburbs of Vienna, it was far removed from the cabals and intrigues of the Italians of the Court theatre. Komorzynski has even asserted that the theatre dedicated itself initially to the furtherance of *Singspiel*, but there is sufficient reason to doubt this. The device on the safety-curtain, for instance, as witnessed and explained by J. Schenk, revealed that the theatre was principally concerned with the reincarnation of the popular comedian, who had been banished from the Kärntnerthortheater in 1776:

> Die Idee des Vorhangs . . . ist artig. Auf der linken Seite sitzt Hans Wurst, mit schwarzem Flor behangen, und betrauert seine Verbannung vom Theater. Weiter in der Mitte des Vorhanges tanzen die Charaktere des wälschen Theaters, Scapin, Pierrot, Harlequin und Dottore einen Reihentanz, aber an Händen und Füssen mit Ketten gebunden; andeutend, dass sie nicht mehr so frei auf dem deutschen Theater erscheinen dürfen. Auf der rechten Seite sieht man den Parnass mit einem Schlagbaum, den ein grämischer, pedantischer Kunstrichter mit einer grossen Rute bewacht und jenen Spassmachern den Eingang auf den Parnass verweigert. Indessen fährt Kasperle, begleitet von Thalien, oben in den Lüften auf einem geflügelten Wagen, dem grämischen Kunstrichter zum Trotz, den Parnass hinauf; was ihm denn jeder gern vergönnt, der billig ist, lebt und leben lässt[28]

Now, of course, the name of Hans Wurst has disappeared and been taken over by Kasperl, played by a gifted comedian Johann von Laroche, the name Casperl first appearing as a comedian in Hafner's second play *Der geplagte Odoardo*. Another source states that Marinelli's theatre was first and foremost concerned with "making one's sides split".[29] The details of Menninger's negotiations with the Emperor and the building authorities also reveal that there was no conscious attempt on the theatre's part to concern itself with performances of *Singspiel*, although the same authority, Franz Hadamowsky, does remark in general and not specific terms, that the repertoire of the theatre contained a large number of *Singspiel* and *Lokalstücke*, the latter being mostly comedies of intrigue, which gave Kasperl opportunity to appear in a variety of disguises.[30] There was in those early years little magic used in the theatrical presentations, hardly any drama or literary comedy. The very first play in the Leopoldstadt-theatre was a Kasperl-burlesque entitled *Aller Anfang ist schwer*.

Financially, Marinelli could not have survived without *Kasperl-possen* and he naturally took advantage of Laroche's almost invincible talent as a popular fool. Only later under Perinet and Hensler did the *Singspiel* flourish in the Kasperltheater.

In his frustration Joseph now turned to Schikaneder, with whose performances in Pressburg he had been favourably impressed, and summoned him to Vienna to perform *Singspiele* in the Kärntnerthortheater, which the latter did successfully from November 5, 1784 until January 6, 1785. The first *Singspiel* to be given was Mozart's *Entführung*, in which the final act of clemency shown towards the leading male and female characters, Belmonte and Constanze, has been attributed by more than one authority to Schikaneder's influence. The *Wiener Zeitung* praised the standard of Schikaneder's company, claiming that it was the best that had been seen in Vienna for years. Unfortunately, dissension in the company, together with Schikaneder's estrangement from his wife, Eleonore, caused the company to disband, leaving Schikaneder in the same position as he had been in at the beginning of his career, as an actor and singer. From April 1, 1785 until February 28, 1786 he was engaged as such at the *Hof- und Nationaltheater*, where there was still a continuous struggle to maintain *Singspiel*. Intrigue was so rife that Schikaneder was whistled off the stage as Essex in Banks's *Die Gunst der Fürsten*, a rôle in which he had had every success on the strolling stage. Komorzynski pointedly remarks that the same part was a favourite of Brockmann's, who acted at the same theatre and was already a firm and zealous favourite there. However, Schikaneder was well received as a singer, in particular as a *Bass-buffo*, when he appeared as Justin in the operetta *Die Dorfhändel*, as Velten in *Die Dorfdeputierten*, and as Jagdl in *Felix der Findling*. As Maler Schwindel he was a success in Gluck's *Pilgrime von Mekka*. During his stay in Vienna Schikaneder applied to the Emperor for a Royal Privilege to build a theatre for the performance of "moral, German plays". The request was promptly granted by Joseph in February, 1786, although Schikaneder was not given permission to build on the glacis, as was his original intention, but in one of the suburbs. The theatre in question, the Theater an der Wien, was not constructed until 1801, but when it was, it was dedicated to the *Singspiel* tradition.[31]

In March 1786 Schikaneder left Vienna and visited Salzburg,

where he remained during May. Here he gave ten performances of German opera, including a *Singspiel* of his own, *Das Urianische Schloss*, which was performed on May 3, and renewed his acquaintance with Leopold Mozart. From there he moved to Augsburg, where he performed mostly *Singspiele* and comedies, and then to Regensburg after the Prince of Thurn had conferred upon him the directorship of the *Teutsches Nationalschauspiel*. The presence of the nobility in Regensburg and their various intrigues against a further attempt to establish German theatre in the face of foreign competition, together with Schikaneder's weakness for the fair sex, which not only provided the anti-German element with more ammunition for its attack but also caused jealousy amongst the female members of the company, made Schikaneder's task impossible after a good beginning. He was fortunate to be summoned to Vienna by his wife, Eleonore, after the death of her lover—Friedel—left the theatre she owned, the Freihaustheater, without a manager. Schikaneder transferred his present directorship to a conscientious member of his company, Jakob Rechenmacher, whose similar patriotic endeavours in Regensburg ended in failure and personal tragedy, and moved to Vienna in June, 1789, where the Royal Imperial Privilege was bestowed upon the theatre on June 21, 1790. With that the foundations were laid for the production of a long series of *Singspiele*, amongst which *The Magic Flute* was to figure prominently in 1791 and the succeeding years. Now Schikaneder came under the direct influence of the inherited traditions of the Old Viennese Popular Theatre, and it was largely due to his efforts that the *Singspiel* form was from 1789 onward firmly embedded in that tradition and developed beyond its still very naïve treatment in the Kasperltheater.

EMANUEL SCHIKANEDER AND THE
VIENNESE *SINGSPIEL* AFTER 1789

Joseph's enterprise, the *Teutsches Nationalsingspiel* was officially
terminated, when the German *Singspiel* company was dismissed
from the Kärntnerthortheater in 1787. One year previously,
Joachim Perinet, Karl Hensler and Wenzel Müller had been
brought together in Karl Marinelli's theatre in the Leopoldstadt
and the *Singspiel*, still virtually in its original awkward state,
began to flourish in a popular suburban theatre, whereas it had
failed dismally in the theatre of the royalty and the aristocracy.

Hadamowsky notes the success accorded to the following *Singspiel* items: *Die Weinlese* (1785) and *Die Weihnacht auf dem
Lande* (1786) by J. Schenk, *Die Gräfin* (1786) by Florian Gass-
mann, *Der gefoppte Bräutigam* (1786), *Apotheker und Doktor*
(1788) and *Hieronimus Knicker* (1789) by Karl Ditters von
Dittersdorf, *Der Rauchfangkehrer* (1786) by Salieri and *La Fras-
catana* (1787) by Paisiello. The greatest success was accorded to
two items by Mozart's rival for popularity in Vienna, Martín y
Soler, *Cosa rara* (1787) and *Baum der Diana* (1788), adapted by
Eberl.[1] It was not until the last decade of the century that Perinet's adaptations from Hafner became famous, such as *Das
Neusonntagskind* (1793) from Hafner's *Der Furchtsame*, *Die
Schwestern von Prag* (1794) from *Der geplagte Odoardo*, *Der
Alte Uberall und Nirgends* (1795) possibly from *Die bürger-
liche Dame*, and *Lustig lebendig* (1796) from *Etwas zum Lachen
im Fasching*. Sonnleithner makes further mention in this respect
of Perinet's successful adaptation of Hafner's *Der beschäftigte
Hausregent* under the title of *Das lustige Beylager*. Hadamow-
sky remarks that by 1794 the performance of *Singspiel* in the
Leopoldstadttheater had passed its best.

The Viennese Theatre Almanac for that year notes that both
the theatres of Marinelli and Schikaneder owed their success

essentially to the genre of *Singspiel*. When Schikaneder arrived in Vienna in 1789 to assume management of the Freihaustheater, he was on this occasion under no obligation to the Emperor to further either the cause of *Singspiel* or of German national drama. Nevertheless the repertoire of his theatre on the strolling stage had earlier proved his interest in, and enthusiasm for, such matters. The strolling stage, and in particular the warm reception accorded to the genre of *Singspiel*, had shown the impresario that the production of *Singspiel*, despite the extra work and outlay, might not be without its financial rewards. After 1789 the repertoire of the Freihaustheater was dominated by *Singspiel*, although Schikaneder's other activities in the theatre at this time should not be ignored.[2]

Professor Deutsch's compilation of first performances in Schikaneder's theatre in 1789, that is, in the new manager's case from June, 1789 to the end of the year, notes eight new, musical items; four comic operas, two *Singspiele*, one opera and one romantic-comic opera.[3] Three of these were written by Schikaneder, two of them were a great success in the same year, whilst the third, *Der dumme Gärtner*, of which six sequels were to follow, was produced on thirty-two occasions before the end of 1789. His programme was not given over entirely to the presentation of popular items, but ranged from the light-hearted *Der dumme Anton* to the more sublime melodrama of Brandes's *Ariadne auf Naxos*. Accordingly the term *Singspiel*, previously quite uniformly applied, divided into various branches of the original form. It was now described according to its textual content and visual grandeur as romantic, heroic, historic, allegoric, comic or magic. Hermann Schletterer notes the same development in *Das deutsche Singspiel*.[4] "Die bisherige knappe Form dehnt sich aus, die Benennungen Singspiel und Operette verschwinden, die grossen romantischen, lyrischen, komischen Opern treten an ihre Stelle."[5]

Schikaneder, in general, does not appear to have been content to reproduce on the Viennese stage the works which were favourites on the strolling stage. Nevertheless there were occasional appearances of the latter. Hiller's *Singspiel*, *Der lustige Schuster*, was performed on August 15, 1790 and prior to that date *Die Lyranten* on February 7.[6] He was very much concerned to redirect his repertoire in the direction of the local Viennese

78

audience and to encourage the introduction of new works to his stage. He therefore offered payment to writers on receipt of any work for his theatre, a promise which gave much greater incentive than the earlier offer from the management of the *Hof- und Nationaltheater* had done in 1778, for in the latter case the writer received nothing until after the work had been given its third performance. The method of payment, of course, did not necessarily encourage the creation of works of a good standard. As late as 1803 the Vienna Theatre Almanac, edited by Joachim Perinet, reported that Schikaneder's theatre, by now the Theater an der Wien, never suffered from lack of material:

> Die gute und prompte Bezahlung der Dichter, denen das Stück gleich nach der Annahme, nicht erst bey oder nach der Vorstellung bezahlt wird, lässt dieses Theater nie an Stücken darben; und daher hat die Direktion nebst den Arbeiten des Herrn Schikaneder, und mehrerer Mitglieder, von einigen der besseren Köpfe des In- und Auslandes Arbeiten zu hoffen, worunter ich Herrn. Richter (Verfasser der Eipeldauer Briefe, und Oesterreichs Rabelais) Herrn Gewey den Verfasser der *Modesitten* (denen bald ein zweyter Theil folgt, und dessen *Seltner Prozess* so sehr gefiel,) mit allem Recht zähle.[7]

Almost inevitably, productions of lesser quality had begun to appear on Schikaneder's stage by 1791, including the various plagiarisms, travesties and adaptations of Georg Karl Giesecke. It is at this time that Schikaneder was said by some to have been bankrupt, or virtually so. Komorzynski, however, Schikaneder's biographer, clearly does not believe this to be true and openly contradicts Dr. Carl Krebs's *Haydn, Mozart, Beethoven* on this point,[8] the latter work taking his authority as Mozart's second biographer Otto Jahn. Jahn's work, of course, did not appear until 1856. Professor Anton Bauer has, however, discovered a note to the effect that Schikaneder was declared bankrupt in 1792,[9] but this is hardly credible when one considers the widespread success which Schikaneder had in the previous year with the several performances of Mozart's *The Magic Flute*, and indeed with other operas and *Singspiele*. On June 21, 1790 Schikaneder had assumed management of the theatre together with Josef von Bauernfeld, but Rommel remarks that Schikaneder was soon able to do without the services of this rich companion and patron.[10] Schikaneder was certainly a great spender, but he was also, apart from occasional minor failures in his lifetime,[11] an enterprising and successful director.

The evidence gathered above tends to support the general truth that it might well have been primarily financial considerations which induced Schikaneder to approach Mozart in the hope that he would set a libretto of his to music. But two other points should not be neglected in this issue, namely, that Schikaneder was already very well acquainted with both Wolfgang and Leopold Mozart, for they had enjoyed many social occasions together in Salzburg in 1780, and Schikaneder, it is reported, had visited Mozart when he was engaged in the Kärntnerthortheater in 1785. Komorzynski even goes so far as to suggest that the seeds for the later fruition of *The Magic Flute* were already in Schikaneder's and Mozart's minds in 1780, but this is, of necessity, pure conjecture. The other point to remember is that Mozart was himself in some considerable financial embarrassment at this time, as one can easily deduce from the several begging letters he wrote to his friend Michael Puchberg between December 29, 1789 and August 14, 1790. The financial transactions between Schikaneder and Mozart at this time should not be allowed to assume proportions over and above their real worth, nor should comments and rumours which lack substantiated authority and supporting evidence be so presented, as they have been, to completely discredit the librettist on the one hand and sanctify the musician on the other. Clearly both men were equally concerned about finance, Mozart more from a personal point of view, Schikaneder from a business point of view. Even the allegations that Schikaneder refused to pay Mozart anything at all for the opera should not be taken too seriously, for there is every evidence to show that Schikaneder was not only honest in his dealings, it may be suspected that he was even over-generous as far as the payment of his company was concerned.[12] No other incident has come to light, which can even remotely suggest that Shikaneder was dishonest.

The *Monatschrift für Theater und Musik* of 1857 contains an article, which is, incidentally, inaccurate in several other details concerning Shikaneder, but which notes that he made no payment at all to Mozart.[13] Mozart himself makes absolutely no mention of any such treatment from Shikaneder, nor do any of the extant theatre almanacs in the ten years or so immediately after the première of *The Magic Flute* refer to it in any way. The same *Monatschrift* remarks rather accusingly that Schikaneder wasn't even present at Mozart's funeral, yet the spirit of this accusation is effectively gainsaid by an article in *Der heimliche Botschafter*,[14] written only eleven days after Mozart's death, in which it was stated that Schikaneder paid the widow the expenses for the funeral on December 7 and announced that Schikaneder was to give a performance of *The Magic Flute* in the next few days, where the proceeds would be given to the widow. The Mozart biography, which appeared many years earlier than Jahn's, namely in 1828, in Leipzig, written by Madame Mozart's second husband, G. N. von Nissen, and edited by herself, levels no accusations of financial inconsiderateness at Schikaneder's head. According to von Nissen, Mozart's enemies spread the rumour that he died with a debt of 30,000 Fl. and on hearing it the Emperor summoned Constanze to appear before him. The widow stated that with a sum of 3,000 Gulden she could clear all outstanding debts and accordingly the Emperor said he would give his support to a concert of the works Mozart left. In von Nissen's own words Mozart was cheated, not by Schikaneder, but by "ein gewisser und ziemlich berühmter Kunsthändler".[15]

The phrase which is placed in Schikaneder's mouth in the *Monatschrift* of 1857, at the moment when he was supposed to have approached Mozart about writing the opera, now becomes clear. Schikaneder is said to have remarked: ". . . Nur du kannst mich retten. Der Kaufherr H. hat mir ein Darlehen von 2,000 Fl. zugesagt, wenn du mir eine Oper schreibst. . ."[16] It would thus appear that whatever deception took place, Schikaneder was not directly concerned with it, but that the third party, the money-lender, was.

Schikaneder's theatres on several occasions produced theatrical and musical items by Mozart, Haydn, Süssmayer and Beethoven. Nevertheless, despite this more serious approach to music, and the large and effective orchestra which the theatres maintained, the almanac of 1794 insisted that the *Singspiele* in the Leopoldstadttheater were frequently more attractively presented than in Schikaneder's.[17] The material for the *Singspiel* of the latter theatre was, however, very much superior. The antithesis of two theatres competing against each other in the suburbs of the city continued to stimulate local interest in the *Singspiel,* and virtuosi and composers became more numerous in the city. There was an upsurge of texts in German, although foreign ones were never completely neglected. Nevertheless even the latter Schikaneder had translated into German before they were performed.[18] Viennese dialect was frequently heard in the theatre, being well suited to the exponents and exposition of comedy, and the dialects of Swabia and Salzburg did not go unrepresented. Later, dialect was frequently used in the suburban theatres to portray character and Schikaneder was one of those responsible for the attempt to elevate the tone of the popular theatre in this way. Komorzynski's summary illustration of the manipulation of Swabian to these ends underlines the traditional inheritance of the suburban theatres. Thus a Swabian snail-dealer was to be found in the works of Joseph Kurz, a Swabian cook in Hafner, and Schikaneder added to the tradition a Swabian cobbler in his *Lokalstück, Das abgebrannte Haus* (1792).[19]

In 1796 in addition to the material which Schikaneder's theatre offered, there were signs in the almanac of that year that Marinelli's theatre was not necessarily concerned overmuch with the development of the *Singspiel* beyond its originally naïve state. The almanac of 1796 adds to its list of actors and actresses for Marinelli's theatre a number of male and female singers from the manager's *Singschule* and mentions an orchestra of thirty musicians. In the same almanac Schikaneder's theatre is found beneath the heading *Deutsche Oper* and his male and female singers are not merely an accessory to the cast-list, but occupy an important place in it. The designation of chorus members as *Choristen* is to be found under Schikaneder's theatre, but not under Marinelli's, and this assumes some significance, when one considers how frequently in his "operatic" work for the popular stage Schikaneder employed a full chorus actively and gave it an integral part in the plot both musically and textually. This was, in many respects, a natural development from the *Massenszenen* inherited from the baroque opera in Vienna earlier in the century.

From 1789 Schikaneder's repertoire offered an unusual degree of variety. In 1789 he commissioned Paul Wranitzky, the Court Musician for the reputedly good orchestra of the *Hof- und*

Nationaltheater, to write a romantic-comic opera for him, which resulted in *Oberon*, *König der Elfen*, with a libretto adapted from Christoph Martin Wieland by Karl Ludwig Giesecke. This already signified a departure from the original form of *Singspiel*. Mozart was a frequent visitor to Schikaneder's theatre, particularly during the time immediately following the first performance of *The Magic Flute* on September 30, 1791. After Mozart's death Schikaneder continued to produce others of his works in the Freihaustheater. He apparently recognized at this stage the inviolability of Mozart's music, yet could not afford his libretti the same privilege. *Don Juan* was performed on November 5, 1792, Da Ponte's text having been adapted and translated into German by Christian Heinrich Spiess. The same librettist suffered a similar fate on August 19, 1794, when the comic opera *Die Schule der Liebe, oder—So machen sie's alle* appeared as an adaptation by Giesecke of Mozart's *Così fan tutte*. The latter was followed on September 6 by *Die Entführung aus dem Serail*—with the text from which it was originally adapted by C. G. Stephanie, by Christoph Friedrich Bretzner. Stephanie's name is not even acknowledged. In the light of Mozart's insistence that Stephanie should make considerable alterations to Bretzner's original text, the wisdom of Schikaneder's decision on this matter must be doubted, although it cannot be forgotten that Mozart also prompted Stephanie to revise his work. Other works by Mozart which Schikaneder performed in his theatre were *Der Schauspieldirektor*, which was given on July 15, 1797, *La Clemenza di Tito*, on September 4 1798, and *Eine kleine Freimaurer-Kantate* (K.623.), probably with words by Schikaneder.[20]

In addition to several productions of opera and *Singspiel*, Deutsch's compilation of performances in Schikaneder's theatre reveals a number of orchestral and instrumental concerts and mention is also made of the occasional recital. Compared with that of Marinelli's theatre, the repertoire is decidedly "heavy". Nunziato Porta's heroic-comic opera *Der Ritter Roland* was revised in German by Gierscheck and given on January 9, 1792. One of Haydn's London symphonies was played in the theatre in 1796 between the two acts of Süssmayer's *Moses*, and the national hymn by Haydn, *Lied an den Kaiser* was sung by the audience on February 12, 1797, prior to the evening production to celebrate the birthday of Franz II. Gluck also maintained his place in Schikaneder's repertoire.

Contemporary musicians, albeit lesser known ones than Mozart and Haydn, such as Henneberg, who had conducted the theatre's orchestra as it was rehearsing for *The Magic Flute* in Mozart's absence, Teyber, who composed the music to Schikaneder's heroic opera *Alexander* (1801) and comic opera *Pfändung und Personal arrest* (1803), Peter von Winter, composer of the sequel to *The Magic Flute*, *Das Labyrinth* (1798), Benedikt Schack and Thaddäus Gerl, Stegmeyer, Haibel—who wrote the music to Schikaneder's very successful *Der Tyroler Wastel* (1796)[21]—Süssmayer, composer of *Der Spiegel von Arkadien* (1794), and Ignaz Ritter von Seyfried, like Süssmayer a pupil of Mozart's, who wrote the music to his magic operas *Untreue aus Liebe* (1805), *Der Löwenbrunn* (1797), *Die Ostindier vom Spittelberg*, and *Mina und Peru* (1799),[22] received especial encouragement from Schikaneder and his singers too were rewarded for their efforts by the financial benefits from occasional performances. One notable concert on October 27, 1798, included works by Mozart, Haydn and Beethoven. It consisted of four arias by Mozart, one of them, "In diesen heil'gen Hallen" sung by K. L. Fischer, from *The Magic Flute*, the overture to the same opera, Beethoven's First Piano Concerto in C Major, op. 15, played by the composer, and '*Die beliebte Sinfonie*' by Haydn as the finale.[23]

Throughout this period there was, of course, a constant need for Schikaneder to exhort his own people to write and compose for the theatre, and, as a result, numerous works appeared which bore the names of the impresario himself or of other members of the company. Castelli's memoirs illustrated how much the intensive work preparatory to actual production on stage made the theatre a hive of industry. On occasion the pressure of work was so great that the music had to be handed out to more than one composer at the same time. Mozart had already participated in this style of working in 1783 when he wrote for the recently instituted *Teutsches Nationalsingspiel*, and he did so again when he shared the music to Schikaneder's *Der Stein der Weisen* with Schack and Gerl. This practice was certainly not uncommon in Vienna, but it should be understood that it could be quite properly applied in creating the music of the *Singspiel*, which was, at least in its original state, very simply conceived with no unity of musical style demanded throughout the work, but that it could not be properly applied when writing the libretto, for it was simply not a practical proposition and would waste instead of saving time. Inevitably it was rumoured that Schikaneder asked a third party, a certain Cantes, to write his lyrics for him, but even Castelli, who was not over indulgent as far as Schikaneder was concerned, had the grace to nip such rumours in the bud by making note of Schikaneder's quick and fertile imagination in the writing of libretti, a quality which Seyfried also remarked upon. Schikaneder never experienced any difficulty in writing verse on the strolling stage, so that it is hard to imagine him having any difficulty in Vienna. Nevertheless the rumour which Castelli tried to scotch in the first volume of his memoirs (1781 to 1813) reappeared in the *Monatschrift für Theater und Musik* of 1857, alongside other points concerning the Schikaneder-Mozart relationship, which, for the most part, can be easily proved untrue.

If one may judge success by quantity of performances, Schikaneder must have ranked in the last decade of the century as the most successful librettist in Vienna. During his residence in the Freihaustheater the twelve most notable successes, which Deutsch has listed in his compilation, included eight of Schikaneder's own. From 1791 until the closing down of the theatre in 1801, *The Magic Flute* achieved 223 performances, *Der Tyroler Wastel* 118 performances from 1796, *Der Spiegel von Arkadien* 98 performances from 1794, *Die Waldmänner* 96 performances from 1793, *Babylons Pyramiden* 64 performances from 1797, *Das Labyrinth* 34 performances in 1798, *Der Königssohn aus Ithaka* 29 performances in 1795 and *Der Wundermann am Rheinfall* 26 performances since 1799.[24]

After offering for more than a decade a programme of unusual variety Schikaneder applied to the Emperor for permission to make use of the royal privilege which had been granted him in 1786 by Joseph II, but of which he had then been unable to take advantage. His intention was to build a new theatre on a different site on the other side of the river Wien. His application was granted in the terms of the original agreement, whereupon Freiherr von Braun, Schikaneder's enemy and director of the *Hof-und Nationaltheater* from 1794 to 1806, sought to upset his plans, insinuating that Vienna could not support another theatre without taking some of the custom away from his own establishment. Braun's legal argument was that the Imperial Court had forbidden the further building of theatres in the city and its environs in 1794 and Schikaneder's application ran contrary to it. The Court, however, discounted this argument, stating that Schikaneder's original grant dated from 1786 and was therefore prior to the Decree of 1794.[25] Other arguments which apparently persuaded the Court to look with favour on Schikaneder's application were the impresario's prompt insistence that the construction of a new theatre would bring employment to a large number of people, and the important consideration that lack of such a theatre, for the Freihaustheater was having to be demolished, would bring discontent to the lower class.[26]

If certain inferences in *Thespis*, the occasional play with which Schikaneder closed the Freihaustheater on June 12, 1801, had any foundation in fact, as it seemed they had, a threat to the continued existence of the Freihaustheater must have made itself felt before Schikaneder decided to build. Certainly Freiherr von Braun strove to discredit Schikaneder in the eyes of the Viennese public and of the Emperor and so intent did he seem to be on bringing discredit on Schikaneder that he gave what turned out to be a very shoddy performance of *The Magic Flute* in the Stadt-theater and omitted Schikaneder's name on the play-bill.[27] In so far as such attempts were of topical interest, Schikaneder was never slow to spring to his own defence in seeing the conflict in terms of theatrical representation, as was also shown in his play *Hanns Dollinger* (Regensburg, 1788), so that ultimately the situation was resolved, at the very least, in terms of popular appeal and good box-office.[28]

Kalistenes, in the play a member of the senate, is a character moved by avarice. Although it is no personal dislike, but merely his desire for financial gain which prompts him to eject Thespis, that is, Schikaneder, from the theatre and from the city, he is suddenly shaken from his impersonal nonchalance when Schikaneder, after most proper and circumspect enquiries, agrees to engage Pistenes—unknown to him, the son of Kalistenes— in his theatre. Further unsavoury facts about Kalistenes are divulged which inflame the situation. Eventually Thespis and his followers have no choice. They must cross the river and head for Athens, that is, their new site on the other bank of the Wien,

86

although evil rumours already precede them there. The final quartet on the last night of the theatre's existence, thanks the audience of the Freihaustheater for its support and asks for it to be continued in the new Theater an der Wien, which was to be opened on the following day, June 13, 1801:

Der Weg ist nicht zu weit,
Der Fluss auch gar nicht breit,
Ein Sprung und Ihr seyd da![29]

The day on which the new theatre opened Schikaneder remained in the part of Thespis and travelled on his cart to his next abode.

The dedication of the new theatre, which was witnessed on the safety curtain, was in the form of a design depicting Tamino fleeing before the serpent. The tableau, the opening picture of *The Magic Flute*, recalled Schikaneder's greatest success and marked the musical dedication of the Theater an der Wien. It has been suggested, however, that the tableau represented Schikaneder fleeing from his generous and rich patron, Zitterbarth, without whose financial assistance the construction of the theatre would have been impossible.[30] Apart from the fact that discord in the management of a theatre is not the appropriate advertisement for its future prosperity, other evidence would refute such an interpretation. In *Thespis Traum*, the short pageant with which Schikaneder opened the new theatre before the fuller performance of his new opera *Alexander*, Schikaneder spoke of his friendship with Zitterbarth, whilst Perinet, even later in 1803, listed the latter amongst Schikaneder's friends.[31] Moreover disagreements and arguments, which certainly did arise between the two and possibly resulted from Zitterbarth's ignorance of theatrical matters, occurred only after the safety-curtain had been hung.[32]. In view of the import of *Thespis*, it is more than likely that the serpent symbolized the vindictive Herr von Braun.

Thespis Traum provided a theatrical link between the closing of the one theatre and the opening of the other. Thespis was now revealed on stage as Schikaneder the impresario, who then alluded to the various obstacles which had confronted him in the creation of the Theater an der Wien and thanked the Court for surmounting them:

87

Wo war ich? Wo bin ich? Wahrlich, das war mein schwerster Traum, aber auch mein herrlichstes Erwachen meiner ganzen Lebenszeit. (*Deutet auf die Büsten.*) Diese drey Denkmahle trug ich längst schon in meinem Herzen, und sollen ewig unauslöschlich in meiner dankbaren Seele wohnen. Nehmet meinen Dank, Ihr Grössten, Ihr Gütigsten auf dieser Erde! Ohne Euch, wo wäre ich nun? Auch Euch, Ihr Grossen, die Ihr am Ruder des Staates waltet, Euch unbestechbaren Richtern, dank' ich demuthsvoll für Eure Huld, für Eure Gnade, für Euren gerechten Anspruch. Dank dem ganzen verehungswürdigen Publicum, für ihre Unterstützung, für ihre Theilnahme meines Schicksals. Dank' dem Freunde, den ich aus Bescheidenheit nicht nennen kann, nicht nennen darf—der mir bisher seine hülfreiche Hand both. Seit ich Thaliens rauhe Bahn betrat, fand ich manchen rechtschaffenen Biedermann, aber, der so was Grösseres für einen Freund wagt, muss eine edles Herz besitzen. Also, meinen öffentlichen Dank auch ihm! O dass es mir—dass es uns allen gelingen möchte, Vergnügen und Freuden Euch zu bringen, Ihre hohen Gönner! dies ist das Schönste, was wir wünschen können, wenn der Mann nach seinen Berufsgeschäften sich unserer Bühne naht, und seine Seele bey uns erheitert; Wir wollen ja gerne, ich verspreche es hier feyerlich, wenn wirs vermögen, Euch nach Möglichkeit zu zerstreuen. Haben wir diesen Zweck erreicht, dann ist dieser Tempel—mein Glück—auf Felsen gebaut.[33]

The same evening an heroic opera, *Alexander*, was performed. The libretto was by Schikaneder and the music by Franz Teyber. Schikaneder had first of all asked Beethoven to write the music, but, after beginning work on the opera, the latter eventually declined.[34] It has been supposed that this was on account of the poor quality of the text, although surely Beethoven would have discovered this before he began. Furthermore the libretto, which is available in the Viennese Austrian Library, is not by any means insipid or of poor quality. Indeed, for a writer who was in the main a popular writer, it shows a not inconsiderable sureness of touch. More probably Beethoven declined as a result of his lack of enthusiasm for operatic composition. The rehearsals immediately preceding the opening night were described by Rosenbaum, secretary of the *Theaterliebhaber*, in his diaries and appear to have been chaotic:

Die Konfusion, das Probieren und Arrangieren eines Marsches und der dreiundzwanzig Pferde, wovon drei vor dem Triumphwagen angespannt waren, welcher rückwärts umstürzte und die Sängerin Campi und den Sänger Simoni herauswarf, alles dies liess nicht einmal glauben, dass noch am selben Tage die Vorstellung stattfinden werde.[35]

Castelli also indulged in criticizing the opera, this time from a vocalic point of view, arguing that the vowel sequence "*Du o Alexander . . .*" would cause the audience to yawn. Despite all these criticisms the opera was a success. The form of the opera was that of the German *Singspiel*, but its heroic content was not entirely unrelated to the tone of *opera seria*. The work contained only the minimal attractions of popular comedy, but it gave new perspectives to the rôle of the chorus in opera. *Alexander* had three choruses: of Greek captains and soldiers; of Indian captains, soldiers, and hunters; and of girls, women, squires, people. In one notable scene the Indian chorus rushes about the stage, singing and searching for Alexander and Kiasa at the same time and in the following scene, the final scene of Act II, Schikaneder ends the opera appropriately with yet another *Massenszene*, this time a triumphal one:

(*Freye Gegend vor der Stadt Bezira, welche rückwärts zu sehen ist. In der Mitte steht eine Triumphpforte; die Coulissen sind eine Allee von Palmbäumen, Hephestion marschiert auf mit Alexanders Heer. Durch die Pforte aus der Stadt kommen indianische Völker, Grosse des Reichs, Damen und Volk, dann Alexander, die Königin und der Prinz; vor diesen tanzen Mädchen und Knaben, und streuen Blumen aus. Das Heer des Alexanders und die Indianer küssen sich untereinander.*)

CHOR

Es erschalle durch die ganze Welt,
Unser Jubel! unsre Freude!
Kiasa leb'! Es leb' der grösste Held!
Immer dauernd so wie heut.
Er gab uns den goldnen Frieden,
Götter haben ihn beschieden,
Uns zur Freude, uns zur Lust,
Euch schlägt dankbar unsere Brust! . . .[36]

True love again finds the solution to the dramatic problem and the opera still cannot break away completely from its popular inheritance. The portrait finds a place among the stage properties, and a sort of popular comedian, Ridoll, serves the Indian cause, being designated a Moor, and keeper of the monkeys and parrots. The content of some of the songs reiterates the traditional *Mann und Weib* theme.

Schikaneder did not long remain the proprietor of the theatre, which—on account of the splendour of its interior decoration, possibly also on account too of the technical innovations which Schikaneder had introduced and which enabled scene changes to be made in record time for that period—came to be known as "Das Wunder an der Wien", for he was bought out according to the terms of the agreement by Zitterbarth.

The latter assumed control of the theatre on July 1, 1802, after it had completed a very succesful year, both musically and financially. From that time until February 14, 1804, Schikaneder retained his authority as director of the theatre. For further services to the theatre he was well rewarded. In addition to being paid 100,000 Gulden for his shares in May, he received a further 400 Gulden for an opera and 200 for a comedy. Both he and his wife received 50 Gulden each time they appeared on stage.[37] Freiherr von Braun, who assumed management of the theatre from February 15, 1804 until December 13, 1806, had in that time to suffer the humiliation of recalling Schikaneder to save the theatre from bankruptcy. Following Sonnleithner from September 1, 1804 until December 31, 1806, Schikaneder assisted his former enemy.[38]

Professor Bauer's chronological list of performances in the Theater an der Wien reveals a preponderance of works by Schikaneder, amongst them an increasing number of *Lokalstücke*. Schikaneder persevered too with comic opera. The production of the second part of *The Magic Flute*, *Das Labyrinth*, possibly a bid to outmanœuvre Goethe who similarly intended producing such a sequel,[39] was so successful in its splendour that *The Magic Flute* had to be restaged to avoid being set at a disadvantage.[40] The success of this work continued, and it was frequently, although not always with the desired effect, performed outside Vienna. *Der Tyroler Wastel* maintained its popularity but *Der Wundermann* and *Babylons Pyramiden* were comparatively only moderate successes. A further four musical items appeared by Schikaneder in 1802, *Tsching, Tsching, Tsching*, a three-act *Singspiel* with music by Haibel, *Proteus und Arabiens Söhne* with music by Seyfried and Stegmayer, *Konrad Langbart* von *Friedburg*, a three-act *ritterliches Singspiel* with music by Henneberg, and a relic of 1794, *Der Spiegel von Arkadien*, a two-act heroic-comic opera with music by Süssmayer.

Other comic operas continued to appear until 1806 but Schikaneder's popularity and the popularity of the genre was declining. Brave, but not very successful attempts were made to maintain the high musical attainment of the theatre. During this period Beethoven's works appeared at the theatre, including the first performance of his oratorio, *Christus am Ölberg*, on April 5, 1805, and of *Fidelio* on November 5 of the same year. The latter was judged a failure by the *Allgemeine Musikalische Zeitung*, the same paper which had condemned Schikaneder earlier and was to do so again later. Beethoven's Violin Concerto in D major, op. 61 was performed on December 23, 1806.[41]

It was during this time that Beethoven had complained about the slackness of rehearsals at the theatre, but Komorzynski would insist that things of greater historical import were then making themselves felt in Vienna. News of Napoleon's crushing victory over General Mack at Ulm reached Vienna on October 20, 1805, which would give the fickle populace ample cause for indifference towards Beethoven, as it would for dislike of Schikaneder, who throughout his life in the theatre had looked upon his work as virtually a national, German enterprise. In the 1799 publication of his letters, the Eipeldauer (i.e. Joseph Richter) had given voice to the city's apprehension with regard to the advance of the French army. In one place he notes that the French have crossed the Rhine, then "alles plaudert französisch". He further remarks on the horrors perpetrated by the French in the Tyrol, news of its having by then reached Vienna, and mentions that Schikaneder's performance of *Die Scharfschützen in Tyrol* donated 500 Fl. to the cause of the unfortunate Tyroleans.[42] By this time even Wranitzky's *Oberon*, which had been so successful in 1789, was clearly out of favour with the Viennese audience. Schikaneder's *Der Tyroler Wastel*, which had met with an overwhelming success in the last decade of the eighteenth century, suddenly found itself whistled off the stage. *Swetards Zaubertal* managed to impress the audience from the point of view of its lavish scenery, but the libretto was described as nonsense. Apart from the apparent exhaustion of Schikaneder's originality, several other factors over which he had no control contributed to his downfall.

The recorded opinions of the Viennese audience at that time suggested that some new style of entertainment was required. Schikaneder was no longer new, nor was the genre *Singspiel*, for it had also by this time appeared in such numbers from Schikaneder, Perinet, and Hensler, that the freshness had been taken from its appeal. It might even be suspected that the extreme lavishness of Schikaneder's later productions reflected already the approaching insanity in which he died on September 21, 1812. Indeed, as early as November 21, 1795, criticisms were heard which might have indicated a certain unsoundness of mind. On that date the *Rheinische Musen* condemned the première of Schikaneder's *Der Höllenberg oder: Prüfung und Lohn*, music by J. Wölffl, as "a confusion of the strangest ideas imaginable".[43] When Napoleon's army advanced toward the city in 1809, it ravaged Nussdorf, where Schikaneder had his private home and possessions, and left him in poverty.[44] By 1810 French opera was once again firmly ensconced in the Austrian capital, and, what must have been harder to bear, in the Theater an der Wien, which had promised so much.

6

SCHIKANEDER'S VIENNESE *SINGSPIELE* PRIOR TO *THE MAGIC FLUTE*

According to the various illustrations of audience reactions in the three publications of the *Eipeldauerbriefe*,[1] Schikaneder now had to cater for more particular tastes than those with which he had been familiar as the manager of a company on the strolling stage. Hence the naïvety of the series of *Singspiele* by Hiller and Weisse prevented their lasting inclusion in the repertoire of Schikaneder's two theatres and also the Kasperltheater. In 1790 he performed Hiller's *Der lustige Schuster* and his own *Die Lyranten* in the Freihaustertheater but little more was heard of either of them.[2]

From the beginning of his residence in the city Schikaneder offered Kasperl, the extremely successful, popular comedian of Marinelli's theatre, serious competition by creating his own popular figure, Anton, whose part he played himself. The impact of Schikaneder's Anton on the Viennese audience was such that, in all, seven *Antonstücke* were produced between the years 1789 and 1795.The first of these was the most successful and had its première on July 12, 1789. The rest of the series, however, do not appear to have been particularly impressive, for none of the seven *Singspiele* appeared again after 1795, and the seventh was performed only twice, by dint of which Rommel concludes, perhaps quite rightly, that they were a failure. The series consisted of: *Der dumme Gärtner aus dem Gebirge oder die zween Anton, Die verdeckten Sachen,* first performed on September 26, 1789, *Was macht der Anton im Winter?,* first performed on January 6, 1790, *Der Frühling oder Anton ist noch nicht tot,* first performed on June 18, 1790, *Anton bei Hofe oder das Namensfest,* first performed on June 4, 1791, *Der Renegat oder Anton in der Türkey,* first performed on September 15, 1792, and *Das Haus im Walde oder Antons Reise nach seinem Geburtsort,* first performed on January 6, 1795. On June 6, 1791, Mozart went to Schikaneder's theatre to see *Anton bei Hofe,* but made no comment, whereas he spoke in most deprecating terms of a performance of Perinet's *Kaspar der Fagottist* which he saw in the Kasperltheater on June 11.[3]

Most of the above *Singspiele* are lost, but the Viennese Austrian National Library possesses the text of the arias from the first three *Antonstücke.* These are of some importance in so far as they reflect both Schikaneder's indebtedness to the various branches of the German theatre and bridge the gap between the popular comedians of his acquaintance on the strolling stage and the Papageno figure of 1791. Thus Act I of *Der dumme Gärtner,* which combines the effect of dawn breaking with the music and song from a chorus of peasants, is very reminiscent of Weisse's *Lottchen am Hofe* and the pastoral bliss which it too depicts in the first act. The first scene also contains a Duchess Josepha, who is slumbering in a summer-house, which evokes the nobler proportions of Mozart's *Hochzeit des Figaro.* Anton's father, Redlich, moralizes against the dangers of passion, thus fulfilling a similar function to Hafner's Herr Redlich in his comedy *Die bürgerliche Dame,* whose name he has possibly taken. In the true consciousness of class, which characterized contemporary Vienna, Josepha bemoans her high-born standing, whence, despite her love, she cannot offer the lowly Anton her hand. Only the dream can realize her wishes:

Arie

Auch im Schlummer seh' ich dich
Trauter Jüngling noch vor mir
Anton! ganz umschwebst du mich
Meine Seele spricht mit dir,
Nannt' dich mein, auf ewig mein;
Aber da erwach' ich kaum,
O so seh' ich leider ein;
Ich besass dich nur im Traum.
Wie verhasst ist mir mein Stand,
Der dich mir auf immer raubt,
Der die hochgebohrne Hand
Meines Gleichen mir entwandt.[4]

However, two songs by Redlich reveal that his son's origins are in fact not too humble after all. Anton as a popular comedian is more akin to the naïve peasant of the *Singspiele* of the strolling

94

stage than to the more forthright Hans Wurst of the Old Viennese Popular Theatre. Like Gürge[5] in Weisse's *Lottchen am Hofe*, and occasionally Barthel[6] in *Der Dorfbarbier*, Anton becomes a victim to the powers of love, where the Viennese Hans Wurst tended to hold himself aloof from it, merely regarding a third party's—usually the hero's—experience of it as a further opportunity for the practice of his comedy. Anton succumbs to his feelings for Josepha and his despair is sincerely founded. But like the Viennese comedians of the popular theatre he is brought by his predicament to the brink of suicide. Papageno's approach to his suicide in *The Magic Flute* in 1791, two years later, has much in common with Anton's plight, although it is felt that the latter is rather more ambitious in the part he plays, almost striving for heroic recognition:

Arie des Gärtner Sohns

O Nacht! viel schwärzer als die Hölle
Tod und Verzweiflung wütet hier,
Kein Lichtstrahl dämmert durch die Hölle
Des aufgethürmten Grams in mir.

Ich bin das Opfer meiner Liebe.
Mich foltert unnennbarer Schmerz,
O fühltst du doch meine Triebe!
Vergebens fühlet sie mein Herz.

Es ist kein Rath, ich bin verloren,
Verloren ist schon mein Verstand,
Zum Jammer war ich stets gebohren,
Willkommner Tod! gieb mir die Hand.

Hinab zum Bach bebend,
Dass kein Gehirn ins Wasser spritzet;
So hat dein Leid ein End.

Fort! Anton fort! wanke nimmer,
Was nüzt mein banges Zaudern,
Was nüzt das Klagen mir,
Josepha! Vater! lebet wohl![7]

In *Die verdeckten Sachen*, however, Anton immediately assumes a completely popular rôle and forgets his delusions of grandeur. Now it would appear that Schikaneder was being influenced more by the traditions of the Old Viennese Popular Theatre than by the popular comedians of his acquaintance on the strolling stage. Anton is now a completely farcical figure and voices his playful thoughts in a manner which places him within the line of development from the early Hans Wursts of Stranitzky and Prehauser to the Papageno of 1791 and those who followed him:

> Wie oft locken Weiber die Männer in d' Falle,
> Belügen, betrügen, das können sie alle,
> Ich kriege den Schlagfluss, das Fieber vor Galle,
> O Weiber! O Weiber! O Weiber!...[8]

Having attempted to break the bounds of class and abduct Josepha, Anton, having failed, declares that he will eat himself to death. Further proof that Anton is no longer a sentimentalist, but merely a popular fool is afforded by the text of an aria which Mozart set to music for Schikaneder: "Ein Weib ist das herrlichste Ding auf der Welt"...[9] The same song provides evidence of Schikaneder's concern to provide his audience not only with popular appeal in the manner of grotesque humour but also by way of items of topical interest. The song is interrupted accordingly:

> Ein Weib ist das herrlichste Ding auf der Welt,
> Wer's leugnet, dem schlag ich, dass d'Goschen ihm schwellt...
>   *(Als der Kourier wegen dem Sieg des Prinzen von Koburg*
>   *einreitet.)*
> Man hört ja fast täglich was Neu's in der Welt
> Besonders von unsern Soldaten im Feld
> Nächst hab' ich, wie ich in die Stadt wollte geh'n
> In schön roten Janckerln viel Reuter geseh'n,
> Die machten treng, teng, teng, und schnalzten brav drein
> Da fragt' ich den einen, wozu soll diess seyn?
> Der sagte, dass Koburg der mächtige Held
> Dem Türken geschlagen, dass die Goschen ihm schwellt.[10]

Perhaps the most appropriate advertisement of Anton's liberation from the sentimental comedy of the strolling stage, and his subsequent subservience to the cause of the Viennese popular comedians, occurs in the third play of the Anton series, *Was macht der Anton im Winter?* The pseudo-heroic Anton of *Der dumme Gärtner* has disappeared in exchange for a comedian who is more vital and realistic in his approach to what for him are the absurdities of life:

96

Papageno, by Ignaz Alberti, from the first programme-book.

PAPAGENO. *Hier meine Schönen, übergeb ich meine Vögel.*
Dritter Auftritt 104?

Sie sind vorbey die guten Zeiten
Als ich noch frey und ledig war
Da durft' ich nur für mich arbeiten
Jetzt schreyt mir bald die kleine Waar
Und bald das Weib die Ohren voll
Beym Sapperment, das ist zu toll. . .[11]

So positive and unemotional is Anton's decrying of the married state, that it could have been uttered by Stranitzky.

Hitherto it has been assumed that Schikaneder's magic opera *Der wohltätige Derwisch*, with music, as far as is known, by "Benedikt Schack, Thaddäus Gerl, and others", was not performed until 1793. However, the printed edition of the text bears the date 1791, and it would therefore seem possible for the work to have been performed before *The Magic Flute*, especially as it was the practice of the contemporary theatre to perform plays in order to gauge their potential success before having them printed. Komorzynski has placed its première in 1793, on September 10, and believes that the work was printed in the same year.[12] An opera of similar mould, *Der Stein der Weisen*, with music by Mozart, Benedikt Schack and Thaddäus Gerl, was performed quite definitely before the première of *The Magic Flute* in 1791. Even without Komorzynski's authority on this point, the fact that *The Magic Flute* was not performed until September 30 and that Mozart, very ill by this time, died five weeks later, on December 5, can only support such an assumption. It is, however, all the more unfortunate that the words and music of *Der Stein der Weisen* are lost, for it would otherwise have cast much light on the several controversies linked with the libretto of *The Magic Flute*. The libretto of *Der wohltätige Derwisch* happily remains extant, but it has still to be established—beyond an uncertain supposition based on one date—that it in fact appeared before *The Magic Flute*. (It is quite possible that it did, but nothing can be definitely supposed as there is insufficient evidence.) Its text is nevertheless clearly the product of the tradition, from which arose the libretto of its more immortal contemporary.

In the manner of the Viennese popular theatre of Hafner's and Schiebeler's day, the hero, Sofrano, is discovered at the beginning of the opera searching for his heroine, Zenomide. The princess, however, is false at heart, and has developed a few stages further than say Hafner's Angela in *Megära* in her villainy. The

Dervish priest, unknown to Sofrano, is his father and plays a rôle very similar to that of Alkantor in Hafner's *Der Furchtsame*. The Dervish, who is being persecuted by Abakuf, the Shiek of Basora, thus helps to lay the foundations for a typically popular, and incidentally, Hafnerian revelation scene. The Dervish places his treasure in the hands of his hitherto very immature son, and the latter foolishly believes that it will buy him the love of the princess:

> Welche nie empfund'ne Freude
> Lieb und Reichthum krönt mich heute
> Mich beglückt bey Gut und Geld
> Das schönste Mädchen auf der Welt.
> Lieb und Geld, und Geld und Liebe
> Sind der Menschen höchste Triebe.
> Wahrlich ich bin ausser mir
> Geld und Liebe lächelt mir[13]

Sofrano is warned by the Dervish that the gold will win her hand but not her heart.

When Sofrano, after much typical wandering, and after effective comic scenes by the popular comedians, Mandalino and Mandalina, acknowledges his gullibility, the Dervish reappears and warns him that if he now acts like a man—and here the terminology is very similar to that used by the priest in *The Magic Flute*, when he addresses Tamino—and robs Abakuf of his powers, then he personally will set the garland on his head:

> Sofrano, mein Sohn! Dein Vater spricht mit dir; dein weibisches Betragen wird erwogen und alle Hilfe dir dadurch entzogen, doch willst du siegen, wohl! so sei ein Mann und dring auf deinen Feind mit Allmacht an; ist er der Kraft durch deinen Arm beraubt, dann wind' ich selbst den Lorbeer um dein Haupt. (*Er verschwindet unter Donner und Blitz, die Säule steht wieder wie zuvor.*)[14]

From this point the plot runs its expected course and Zenomide is finally transformed into a good person who glows "in flammender Liebe". Both hero and heroine experience the betterment of character inherent in the majority of Viennese plays of the popular stage and in this compare very closely with the hero and heroine of *The Magic Flute*, Tamino and Pamina. Komorzynski has suggested that the source of the libretto consisted of two legends, *Die Prinzessin mit der langen Nase* and *Der eiserne Armleuchter*, from Wieland's *Dschinnistan*, a collection of fairy-tales.[15]

The so-called "popular" style of music, which occurs occasionally in *The Magic Flute*, reveals the opera's indebtedness to a tradition closely allied to the one which produced the *Singspiele* of Johann Adam Hiller on the strolling stage. Hiller discovered by experience that his Italian schooling in musical composition was a completely irrelevant attribute when writing for the popular stage. Leopold Mozart was very much aware of the limited appeal of his son's music, when he recommended him not to forget popular appeal when composing the music to *Idomeneo*. On December 11, 1780 he wrote from Salzburg to his son in Munich:

> Ich empfehle Dir bey Deiner Arbeit nicht einzig und allein für das musikalische, sondern auch für das *ohnmusikalische Publikum* zu denken. Du weisst es sind 100 *ohnwissende* gegen 10 *wahre Kenner*, vergiss also das sogenannte *populare* nicht, das auch die *langen Ohren* kitzelt.[16]

Mozart replied to the letter five days later, and, in so doing, revealed that he did not treat his father's advice seriously:

> . . . wegen dem sogenannten Populare sorgen Sie nichts, denn, in meiner oper ist Musick für aller Gattungen leute;—ausgenommen für lange ohren nicht.[17]

Certainly it is doubtful what *Idomeneo*, an *opera seria*, contained for the musically "long-eared" members of the Court audience in Munich, but Schikaneder in 1791 was adamant that it should be contained in the music of *The Magic Flute*. It is from such a point of view that sense is made of many of the strange rumours which circulated about the association between Mozart and Schikaneder. Castelli's memoirs, for instance, includes the following in the comments on the Theater auf der Wieden:

> Lächerlich ist, was Schikaneder einem Freunde, der ihm nach der ersten Aufführung der "Zauberflöte" Lobsprüche **über sein** Werk machte, geantwortet haben soll. Er soll gesagt haben: Ja, die Oper hat gefallen, aber sie würde noch mehr gefallen haben, wenn mir Mozart nicht soviel daran verdorben hätte. . .[18]

99

Castelli, of course, has already been shown to be not a very dependable authority, unless his information is confirmed elsewhere. Many other sources, for instance, directly contradict his assertion that Schikaneder couldn't sing. He was the only one to voice this opinion, although critics who were not contemporary, have since joyfully accepted the statement without question, Castelli remaining the sole authority. The above statement contains, however, what might well be a grain of truth, namely, that Schikaneder in fact said what Castelli reported him as saying. Gräffner's memoirs record a statement with similar import,[19] although again it is not impossible that Gräffner had recourse to Castelli. Where Castelli does reveal his shortcomings in the above extract is when he calls the rumour ridiculous, clearly doing his utmost to be fair to Schikaneder. Perhaps the phrase was intended ironically, certainly it could not be construed as an expression of Schikaneder's bitterness, for even the première of the opera was a creditable success, but, whatever its tenor, the statement is a complete affirmation of Schikaneder's character, as illustrated by his biographer and by more contemporary sources, and of his intentions, confirmed elsewhere, that the opera should contain at least some music to appeal to popular tastes. After all Schikaneder, from a financial point of view, was very concerned with the reaction of his audience, more so than Mozart was with the Court audience in Munich.

Wagner was full of praise for the melodic content of *The Magic Flute,* and E. K. Blümml also admired the "leicht ins Ohr fallende Mozartsche Weisen".[20] It appears probable, however, that Mozart alone was not entirely responsible for the melodies of the opera, but that Schikaneder had a hand in the composition of at least three of them. Schikaneder had by this time an intimate acquaintance with the demands of the Viennese audience which visited his theatre, and was well aware of their preference for simple and attractive melodies. To realize his "popular" aims in the production of the opera, he had to be very persuasive with regard to the musician he had chosen to complete the task. That this was achieved without there being any resultant ill-feeling, at least there is no contemporary evidence of it, reflects not only a degree of mutual friendship, but also a certain understanding of each other's art. Komorzynski and Rommel insist that Mozart and Schikaneder worked very closely together in the production of the new opera.[21] The belief that Mozart influenced Shikaneder in the arrangement of the moral issues of the libretto should not be too readily accepted, for more than one source states that the libretto was completed before Schikaneder approached Mozart, and all sources show Schikaneder to be by far the more forceful personality of the two.

Three authorities at least are aware of Schikaneder's participation in the musical composition of the opera: but it must be remembered that Schikaneder's interference resulted from his concern as a talented producer of a suburban theatre, rather than from any innate musicianship. All sources appear to have a measure of agreement in that they either state or strongly infer that the melodies to all the popular songs were the issue of Schikaneder's insistence for this type of appeal. Thus Gräffner's memoirs state:

. . . Mit manchen war er unzufrieden, ein scharfer Censor, aber ein practischer Kopf, der sein Publicum kannte. Hundert Mahl schärfte dieser practische Kopf Mozart dem Genie ein: Nicht so gelehrt, Freund, das ist zu hoch für die Leute; das musst Du einfacher natürlicher machen, und das Genie machte es, wie der Herr Director und der Herr Bruder es verlangte. Das Duett: Bey Männern, welche Liebe fühlen, etc., musste ihm Mozart nicht weniger als vier Mahl abändern, ganz wenden und umstürzen, und dennoch war es dem rigorösen Tactmenschen noch nicht recht. Das ist alles zu gelehrt, entschied er; so will ich es haben, und sang ihm das Duett vor wie er es wollte und brauchte, und—wie Mozart es auch wirklich adoptirte und componirte, so also, wie wir es haben. "Das Duett," erklärte Schikaneder, "ist von mir". (Nicht minder sind auch die meisten Papagenolieder von ihm.)[22]

These memoirs did not appear, however, until 1845, some long time after the première of the opera, and it is quite possible that Gräffner heard the rumours from Castelli, whose first volume of memoirs spanned the years 1781 to 1813. Castelli is more specific than Gräffner and names all three songs of the opera, but the motive he attributes to Schikaneder for the latter's interference, namely that the latter could not sing the more difficult parts which Mozart had intended, has received no support from any other authority and has even been refuted by some.[23]

Schikaneder war ein erbärmlicher Sänger, daher er in seinen Opern die Melodie zu jenen Stellen, welche er selbst zu singen hatte, selbst machte, oder dem Componisten vorschrieb. So sind die Melodien in der *Zauberflöte* zu den Liedern: "Der Vogelfänger bin ich ja," und "Ein Mädchen oder Weibchen", sowie zu dem Duette: "Bei Männern, welche Liebe fühlen" von Schikaneder; Mozart hat sie erst durch sein herrliches Instrumentale zu Kunstwerken gemacht...[24]

Castelli names the songs concerned in rumours of this nature and all of them have the light, catchy melodies which would appeal to a Viennese audience bent on entertainment. Significantly, these three musical items all involve the popular comedian, Papageno, the duet being sung by himself and Pamina. It would therefore appear that by imposing popular melody on the popular comedian, Schikaneder was playing his own part in the musical, as well as the textual, characterization of the opera.[25] Castelli's assumption that the three popular tunes mentioned above were by Schikaneder would attribute to Schikaneder the gift of musical inventiveness, but it should be noted that Komorzynski has related the song "Der Vogelfänger bin ich ja..." to an earlier song by Christian Friedrich Schubart, the "Lied eines Vogelstellers" (1782),[26] with which Schikaneder was most probably acquainted, and that A. Hyatt King has referred to the close similarities between "Ein Mädchen oder Weibchen" and two possible sources, a chorale in 2/2 time by Scandello, and Haydn's *Il mondo della luna*.[27] Further to confirm the rumours mentioned above it is perhaps desirable to refer to an authority, who was considerably earlier than Gräffner, and who was both a contemporary, and from 1798 until 1803 a colleague, of Schikaneder's, Joachim Perinet. In 1801 and 1802 he wrote and published two poetic treatises to the relationship between Mozart and Schikaneder: *Mozart und Schikaneder. Ein theatralisches Gespräch über die Aufführung der Zauberflöte im Stadttheater*, and *Ein theatralisches Gespräch zwischen Mozart und Schikaneder über den Verkauf des Theaters*. In the former, in general terms however, Perinet mentions the same rumours mentioned by Castelli and Gräffner. Since Castelli's memoirs offer a considerable degree of detail, and were not published until 1813, it would suggest that Perinet was not the only source of the rumours, for the latter's eulogy of Schikaneder is phrased only in vague terms:

Ich bekenne, meine Musik hat mir g'rathen,
Wir wussten, alle zwey, was wir thaten:
Du hast mir manche Melodey vorharmonirt—
Freylich hab' ich's hernach erst aufgeführt;
Aber du hast mich zu einer Zeit erwählt,
Wo mich so mancher Charlatan hat geschnellt,
Du hast verstanden, was ich kann, und vermag.
Und warst ein Freund vom ächten Schlag'.
Du gabst mir Gelegenheit mich zu zeigen
Und ich machte deinen Plan mir eigen.
Lache dazu, wenn man jetzt schimpft, oder flucht,
Ich war ja zu haben, warum hab'n's mich nicht g'sucht?
Du hast mich gesucht, und ich hab' dich gefunden,
Wir lieferten was Grosses, mitsammen verbunden:
Da standen sie um mit offenen Mäulern und Nasen,
Und wollten am End' ihr Gift auf dich blasen,
Du warst HIER der Erste, keiner früher,
Du warst der Vater, ich der Erzieher;
Hätte der Vater kein Kind gemacht,
Wär's auch mit der Erziehung gute Nacht. . .[28]

It further appears that Schikaneder's part in the musical composition of the opera was not restricted to the three popular songs alone. A letter from Sebastian Meyer, second husband to Mozart's sister-in-law Madame Hofer, and in 1791 a bass singer in Schikaneder's theatre, records the following comment on a rehearsal of the first encounter in the opera between Papageno and Papagena: Schikaneder shouted down to the orchestra:

> Du Mozart! Das ist nichts, da muss die Musik mehr Staunen ausdrücken, beide müssen sich erst stumm anblicken, dann muss Papageno zu stottern anfangen: Pa-pa pa pa-pa; Papageno muss dies wiederholen, bis endlich beide den ganzen Namen aussprechen.[29]

This item from the letter was recorded by Castelli, and Rommel remarks in his book on the Old Viennese Popular Comedy, that the report originally stemmed from the Weber family, who were not very kindly disposed towards Schikaneder. Castelli also reports that the existence of the priests' march at the beginning of Act II was due to Schikaneder's intervention, for, in the first instance, their entry had no musical accompaniment. No sooner had Schikaneder spotted the deficiency than Mozart sat down and wrote the music there and then. This was at the dress-rehearsal on September 28, 1791, the same day on which Mozart composed the overture to the opera.

The reception of the opera in Vienna, the same city in which in the following decade Beethoven's *Fidelio* was to be regarded as a failure, fully justified Schikaneder's insistence that Mozart should not neglect the popular tastes of his audience. The first act did not win immediate approval on the first night. Mozart was upset as a result of this and in the interval expressed his anxiety for the opera to Schikaneder. The latter calmed him with: "Ich kenne die Wiener besser" and the subsequent act and performances of the opera justified the impresario's confidence, for the audience was delighted. One of the popular melodies became a regular encore, which marked the satisfaction of contemporary Vienna, but Mozart's sense of gratification from the "silent approval" reflects the deeper musical value of his gift to posterity. The following extract is from a letter which Mozart wrote to his wife in Baden, on October 7 and 8, a week after the première and marks the abundant success of the opera:

> Eben komme ich von der Oper; Sie war eben so voll wie allweit. Das Duetto Mann und Weib etc., und das Glöckchen Spiel im ersten Ackt wurde wie gewöhnlich wiederhollet—auch im 2. Ackt das Knaben Terzett—was mich aber am meisten freuet, ist der stille beifall! man sieht recht wie sehr und immer mehr diese Oper steigt.[30]

7

THE MAGIC FLUTE AND ITS DISPUTED
AUTHORSHIP

Brigid Brophy in her *Mozart the Dramatist*, has continued to uphold the belief that the libretto of *The Magic Flute* was the result of collaboration between Schikaneder and a member of his theatre, Karl Ludwig Giesecke.[1] This is at very best a generalization of the truth and because of its lack of exact detail can induce in the reader conclusions which are the opposite of the true ones. Brigid Brophy appears to be contented with the generalization and chooses not to elucidate further. Such misunderstanding of the relationship between Schikaneder and Giesecke is not the original work of Brigid Brophy alone, but was encouraged by the particular emphasis of Otto Jahn's Mozart biography in 1856[2] and perpetuated by E. J. Dent's *Mozart's Opera, The Magic Flute* and *Mozart's Operas: a Critical Study*, in 1911 and 1913. It is significant that Brigid Brophy's book does not include in its bibliography the names of E. Komorzynski, Schikaneder's only biographer, and O. Rommel, the literary historian of the Old Viennese Popular Theatre. The latter's work appeared in 1952, while the latest edition of the Schikaneder biography appeared in the previous year. Each of these authorities has shown, beyond all reasonable doubt, that Schikaneder was the sole librettist of *The Magic Flute*, and although the nature of their evidence cannot be regarded as absolutely final, it indicated a course which recent Mozart research has had to follow in the search for the truth. The first biographer of Mozart, G. N. von Nissen, whose work appeared in 1828, infers that Schikaneder might have been concerned with some financial trickery in selling the text of the opera,[3] but however the truth of these inferences may eventually be established, Nissen makes absolutely no reference to a controversy surrounding the authorship of the opera's libretto. In such a context the name of Giesecke does not appear. Rommel's researches have shown that

Giesecke was an arranger and adapter totally unfitted for the creation of a text such as that of *The Magic Flute*.[4]

In the membership of Schikaneder's Freihaustheater Giesecke was listed as a second-rate actor and arranger. His true métier was academic rather than theatrical and resulted in his eventual appointment of Professor of Mineralogy at Dublin University. Giesecke's works for the stage lacked any originality and consisted in the main of travesties and adaptations of the several plots being circulated in the busy, popular theatres of the city.[5] Plagiarism was, of course, common practice in eighteenth century Vienna and the whole tradition of the theatre, from its establishment in 1712 by Stranitzky to its demise with the death of Nestroy, thrived on the subversion of popular and original material for theatrical ends. The better playwrights of the popular theatres acknowledged their sources, the lesser ones did not. In at least one instance Giesecke belonged to this latter class. Soon after his arrival in Vienna in 1789, Schikaneder commissioned Giesecke to write for him a book for a magic opera. Wranitzky, a leading musician in the Stadttheater and a person who later at least showed a genuine degree of friendship for Schikaneder, wrote the music for the ensuing opera, *Oberon, König der Elfen*, which enjoyed a successful first performance in Schikaneder's theatre on November 7, 1789.[6] In addition to other close textual affinities 12 of its 26 arias were verbatim copies of arias in Sophie Seyler's *Oberon oder König der Elfen*,[7] which was first performed as early as July 1788, before Schikaneder had arrived in Vienna to assume the management of the Freihaustheater. The Seyler version had already met with a measure of success. With the right intentions but with rather misplaced emphasis, Giesecke's roguery has been manipulated to discredit him absolutely,[8] while Schikaneder has had an honesty and warm-heartedness thrust upon him which could never allow such blatant deception. Castelli's memoirs and Perinet's activities as poet and critic uphold the truth of this picture of Schikaneder, but the Oberon episode has a musicological importance far greater than one concerned with the mere exposition of Giesecke's and Schikaneder's characters. Giesecke's version of the Oberon opera refused to acknowledge Sophie Seyler but it did acknowledge Wieland as its source. The earlier opera by Sophie Seyler had already acknowledged Wieland, and as the bulk of

Giesecke's opera was word for word the same as its predecessor of 1788, Giesecke's reference to Wieland cannot prove that he was acquainted with the original. Rather does the episode suggest that Sophie Seyler knew Wieland's *Oberon* and that Giesecke did not. Whatever the final truth of the above argument, the present truth is that Giesecke knew of Wieland, either via Sophie Seyler or as a result of his own reading.

A number of authorities, including Rommel, have come to accept the view that Giesecke was responsible for turning Schikaneder's attentions to Wieland as a possible source for opera libretti. Since it was Schikaneder who commissioned Giesecke to write a magic opera for his theatre, it is not altogether impossible that it was Schikaneder who attempted to direct Giesecke's attentions to Wieland. The Oberon episode leaves considerable doubt as to whether Giesecke even knew Wieland's original and it is perhaps of some importance that Wieland's *Dschinnistan,* which, several authorities insist, provided Schikaneder with the source for his opera, does not contain the Oberon poem which first appeared in 1780. This would tend to separate Giesecke from the sphere of influence surrounding the creation of *The Magic Flute.* Until it has been verified that Giesecke knew either Wieland's *Oberon* or his *Dschinnistan,* his influence on Schikaneder must not be overrated.

Schikaneder certainly appears to have been acquainted with Wieland's *Dschinnistan,* a collection of fairy-tales, edited, adapted, and in some cases written by Wieland, which appeared in Winterthur in 3 volumes between the years 1786 and 1789. The third volume contained a legend by Liebeskind, *Lulu oder die Zauberflöte* which has been widely held as the source of Schikaneder's libretto.[9] Komorzynski and Bauer see *Dschinnistan* as having a wider influence on other magic operas by Schikaneder. Komorzynski believes it to be the inspiration for Schikaneder's *Der Stein der Weisen oder: die Zauberinsel* (1791), *Der wohltätige Derwisch* (1791 or 1793) and *Der Spiegel von Arkadien* (1794),[10] while Bauer supports his view that part two of *The Magic Flute* is from the same source, specifically from *Das Labyrinth* (1798)[11] by a "dear friend" of Wieland's Herr von E.[12] Schikaneder acknowledged some indebtedness to Wieland when he left him 300 Gulden in his last will and testament as the "author of *Dschinnistan.*"[13]

In his Schikaneder biography Komorzynski has noted the playwright's tendency to seize inspiration from an original source and then to write his own play or libretto as it arose from the inspiration. In any age, this is, of course, a fairly widespread habit and should not therefore be used to belittle Schikaneder's achievements. In this manner Schikaneder was influenced by Lessing[14] and by Schiller,[15] to name only two of his several sources, and it is probable that *Dschinnistan* has a similar degree of importance as a source. Some of the legends in the latter collection have very obvious similarities with the libretti of Schikaneder's magic operas, but Schikaneder's methods by no means killed, nor even stultified, the original treatment he gave stories and he was by no means possessed of the plagiaristic tendencies of Giesecke. With all these cases in point, including the comparison between the libretto of *The Magic Flute* and Liebeskind's *Lulu oder die Zauberflöte,* the schema of the story is different and what borrowing there is, is limited in the main to titles of legends, names, places and, occasionally, the magical apparatus of the plot. Thus in its essential story Schikaneder's *Das Labyrinth oder der Kampf mit den Elementen* is very different from *Das Labyrinth* in Wieland's *Dschinnistan.* Schikaneder's version is clearly and explicitly the sequel to *The Magic Flute,* the version in *Dschinnistan* is not. Ideas found in the latter recur in *The Magic Flute* and in the subsequent magic operas but Schikaneder's works are nonetheless originally conceived. It is also to be observed that the libretto of *The Magic Flute* contains features, ideas and machinery which are not to be found in any of the stories of *Dschinnistan,* but which do appear in the abundance of plots of the popular stage. This would tend to diminish Wieland's influence. The popular figures, the attempted suicide and the portrait scene are cases in point. In these instances Schikaneder's libretto is much more similar to Schiebeler's *Lisuart und Dariolette* and to Hafner's *Megära die förchterliche Hexe* than to *Dschinnistan.* Fritz Grandaur further diminishes the significance of this collection in the matter when he indicates the close textual parallels between Schikaneder's libretto and Abbé von Terrasson's academic history *La vie de Séthos,* as translated into German by Matthias Claudius.[16] The diminution of *Dschinnistan's* influence on the creation of *The*

Magic Flute automatically minimizes Giesecke's influence on Schikaneder.

The belief that Giesecke was one of the librettists of *The Magic Flute* arose from the publication in 1849 of an article in *Die Oper in Deutschland* by Julius Cornet.[17] In it Cornet describes a meeting between himself, Giesecke and others, in such a way as to encourage the notion that Giesecke shared in the creation of the opera's libretto. The following remark precedes the description of the meeting, but voices assumptions which are clearly based on that incident:

> Und vor allen die ächt deutsche *Zauberflöte* von Schikaneder und seinen Choristen Giesecke, der ihm den Plan der Handlung, Scenen-Eintheilung und die bekannten naiven Reime machte.[18]

There is no contemporary evidence available to support these assertions. They were made known 58 years after the opera's successful première in 1791 and depended for their existence on a meeting which had taken place 31 years previously. In the first place Cornet's reliability has been questioned,[19] while the three divisions of the above statement reveal ignorance of Schikaneder's creative abilities. It is virtually incredible that Giesecke, who was noted for his lack of originality, could have been in any way responsible for the construction of a plot as rich as that of *The Magic Flute*, unless that plot had been taken directly from Wieland or Sophie Seyler. Castelli allows himself rather disparaging comments about Giesecke's talents: "Herr Giesecke hatte kein eigentliches Fach und spielte was er eben musste..."[20] It is equally erroneous to believe that Giesecke could suggest the division and arrangement of scenes to a man, who, as a result of unusually wide theatrical experience, was extremely knowledgeable as a producer, and in whose works, whatever their literary worth, both before and after *The Magic Flute*, his genius as a "Theatermann" is abundantly evident. It is also unlikely that Schikaneder's vivid imagination would require assistance from Giesecke in the fabrication of rhyme.

The alleged meeting between Cornet and Giesecke occurred in the summer of 1818 in the presence of Ignaz von Seyfried, Korntheuer, Julius Laroche, Küstner and Gned:

> Bei dieser Gelegenheit erfuhren wir denn so vieles aus der alten Zeit; unter Andern lernten wir auch in Ihm (der zu dem damals

hochverpönten Orden der Freimaurer gehörte), den eigentlichen Verfasser der *Zauberflöte* kennen, (wovon Seyfried allerdings eine Ahnung hatte.) Ich erzähle dies nach seiner eigenen Aussage, welche zu bezweifeln wir keine Ursache hatten. Er erklärte sich hierüber gegen uns bei der Gelegenheit, als ich die eingelegte Cavatine aus *Der Spiegel von Arcadien* sang. Viele meinten der Souffleur Helmböck sei Schikaneders Mitarbeiter gewesen. Aber auch hierüber enttäuschte uns Giesecke, nur die Figur des Papageno und seiner Frau gestand Giesecke dem Schikaneder zu.[21]

There is no further evidence to support these claims. Castelli's memoirs establish the fact that the man named by Cornet as Küstner could not have been at the meeting in 1818 for he was dead by that time. Castelli remarks on Küstner's criminal tendencies which drove him to suicide some time within the years covered by Castelli's first volume of memoirs, namely between 1781 and 1813. At the very latest, Küstner was dead 5 years before the supposed meeting which Cornet describes. Ignaz von Seyfried, who according to Cornet had suspected that Schikaneder was not the sole librettist of *The Magic Flute*, was the only other witness left alive in 1849. In 1791, the year in which the opera received its first performance, Seyfried was only 15 years old, as Rommel has pointed out.[22] Seyfried was initiated by Schikaneder in the ways of theatrical musicianship and was subsequently familiar with the impresario's modus operandi,[23] he never refers to these, what must have been startling assertions by Cornet, although he was supposedly present at the meeting in 1818. On the contrary he testifies to the fact that Schikaneder was a prolific writer who had little need of assistance:

Schikaneder sei zwar ohne literarische Bildung, habe aber über eine natürliche Begabung und eine ungemein fruchtbare Phantasie verfügt.[24]

Castelli's memoirs express a similar respect for Schikaneder's capacity for creative work when he scotches a rumour that Schikaneder had sought assistance from a priest by the name of Wüst. It is the lack of that ability in Wüst which induces Castelli to discount the rumour. Joachim Perinet, previously a playwright in Marinelli's theatre, served Schikaneder as writer and actor in the Freihaustheater and Theater an der Wien from 1798 to 1803. As editor of the *Wiener Hoftheateralmanach* of 1803

Perinet contradicts further rumours which were circulating about Schikaneder. It is not impossible that Castelli and Perinet were referring to the same source:

> Hier ist auch ein Gerede zu widerlegen, das sich fast allgemein fälschlich verbreitete, als wäre Schikaneder nicht Vater und eigener Fabrizierer seiner theatralischen Kinder. Es ist erwiesen, dass Plan und Dialogisierung sein Eigen sind, und Herr Winter, der zugleich Inspizient dieses Theaters ist, wird es attestieren, denn nur er und vielleicht er allein kann Schikaneders Hieroglyphen lesen, die er immer zuerst zu kopieren bekommt.[25]

Herr Winter was a member of the company of the Freihaustheater in 1791, the year in which *The Magic Flute* first appeared. He was apparently still in the service of the same theatre in 1794 for he is listed in the *Hoftheateralmanach* for that year as "Winter: gesetzte Rollen". The almanac for 1796 does not mention his name, but in 1803 he appears again as the theatre's stage-manager.

Perhaps as a result of Castelli's and Perinet's interference the rumours died. Nevertheless, that such thoughts should have been in people's minds, requires some further elucidation, as far as this is possible. In the early years of the new century it was known in Vienna that there existed a strong feeling of enmity between Schikaneder, the successful manager of a suburban theatre, and Freiherr von Braun, the envious impresario of the not so successful *Hof- und Nationaltheater*, which had been established in Vienna in 1778. When Schikaneder and his company moved into the new theatre, the Theater an der Wien in 1801, *Thespis*, an occasional play by Schikaneder which he used to close the Freihaustheater, made it quite clear that evil rumours preceded his journey to the other side of the river Wien. Braun had done his utmost to discredit Schikaneder in the eyes of the Viennese public, and even after the Imperial Court had granted Schikaneder permission to build his new theatre, he had sought to have that agreement withdrawn. Schikaneder makes a public reference to Braun's intrigues in *Thespis Traum*, a curtain-raiser on the first night of the Theater an der Wien, although he avoids mentioning his enemy by name:

SCHIKANEDER: Nehmet meinen Dank, Ihr Grössten, Ihr Gütigsten auf dieser Erde! Ohne Euch, wo wäre ich nun? Auch Euch,

Ihr Grossen, die Ihr am Ruder des Staates waltet, Euch unbestechbaren Richtern, dank' ich demuthsvoll für Eure Huld, für
Eure Gnade, für Euren gerechten Anspruch.[26]

Rumours of this nature were doubtless instigated by Braun in
the first place when he gave a wretched performance of *The
Magic Flute* in the Stadttheater and refused to include Schikaneder's name on the play-bill. Perinet comments on these subver-
sive activies of Braun in the almanac of 1803 and in his poetic
eulogy: *Mozart und Schikaneder. Ein theatralisches Gespräch
über die Aufführung der Zauberflöte im Stadttheater,* in 1801.
It is not unlikely that Braun's performance of *The Magic Flute*
took place during the negotiations between Schikaneder and the
Imperial Court.

Under these circumstances it is not altogether suprising that
Schikaneder has since been constantly maligned. Otto Jahn, in
his biography, thus took up Cornet's message, and it gathered
momentum of its own accord. However, the truth of Cornet's
report becomes apparent with the realization that, although
Seyfried did not give any material support to Cornet's observations, he did maintain that Giesecke was the one who turned
Schikaneder's attentions to Wieland. This is most probably true
although the influence of *Dschinnistan* on the creation of *The
Magic Flute* must not be overestimated. In his will Schikaneder
acknowledged Wieland, probably because of the limited influence
the fairy-tales had on a wide range of his magic operas, but
throughout his life-time he made no mention of his gratitude to
Giesecke.

It is in this light that Giesecke can be regarded as "den eigentlichen Verfasser der *Zauberflöte*", that is, he assumed that he was
the real author in that he suggested the source to Schikaneder.
It is also significant to note how the statement found in Cornet
was slightly rephrased by Mozart's biographer Otto Jahn: Cornet used the phrase "den eigentlichen Verfasser"—"the real
author", whereas Jahn uses the words "der Hauptverfasser",[27]
"the main author", which is a not insignificant deviation from
the original. It follows from this that Giesecke's supplementary
assertion that only the figures of Papageno and Papagena were
due to Schikaneder's invention may be true, for the popular figures
do not appear in any of the fairy-tales found in *Dschinnistan*.

Es lebe SARASTRO
Sechzehnter Auftritt I Act.

NATUR

WEISHEIT

VERNUNFT

Finale, Act I; première in Schikaneder's Freihaustheater, 1791; by Geyl and Nessthaler.

Emanuel Schikaneder, by Philipp Richter.

Giesecke, of course, did not realize that there were several other features of the libretto of *The Magic Flute*, which were not to be found in *Dschinnistan*, hence his tendency to overemphasize the importance of Wieland, and subsequently of his own part in the creation of the opera's libretto. The libretto of *The Magic Flute* is essentially the product of the tradition which originated in the Old Viennese Popular Theatre, a tradition in which Schikaneder figured prominently, and Giesecke, the academic jack-of-all-theatrical-trades, hardly at all.

8

THE UNITY OF SCHIKANEDER'S LIBRETTO

At least two recent publications in England have upheld the almost traditional belief that the libretto of *The Magic Flute* is disjointed in its structure.[1] Specifically, but not wholly, it is supposed that the Queen of Night and Sarastro undergo a sudden and unmotivated change of character from good to evil and vice versa. In both cases the works of E. J. Dent appear in the bibliography as the source for this assumption.[2] In neither case is its validity established by reference to an authoritative version of the text. Otto Jahn, whose Mozart biography appeared in 1856, was the first to pose, quite persuasively, the thesis of a belated and clumsy alteration of the libretto. He is also completely ignored.

Otto Jahn's book would in theory have more to recommend it than Dent's, for 1856 appears in time to be much nearer the actual circumstances of 1791 than 1911 and 1913, and yet even Jahn's sources remain somewhat remote from the last decade of the eighteenth century. The nearest he comes in time to the year of the first performance of *The Magic Flute* is 1841[3] and his other three main sources on this particular matter are dated 1849,[4] 1852[5] and 1857,[6] which is in itself most unsatisfactory when he is in the first place seeking to establish such an irregular hypothesis. Much of Jahn's detailed material on the question of an alleged break in the opera's libretto appears to come directly from one of the above named sources, the *Monatschrift für Theater und Musik* of 1857.[7] The article, in addition to its remoteness in time, can be severally attacked for inaccuracies regarding the Mozart and Schikaneder relationship, although where the author keeps to strictly factual information he is generally correct. Mostly he is wrong by inference and by emphasis. One would assume, for instance, from the way in which *Dschinnistan* is mentioned, that the fairy-tale *Lulu oder die Zauberflöte* contained therein, was by Wieland, when in fact it was by Liebeskind. This, of course, is not the place to dissect the article in detail, merely let it be indicated that the source is at the very best a dubious one. But if many questions appear to have been raised in the 1840's and 1850's concerning the authorship of the libretto and its supposed disunity, the years of the immediate environment of the opera, namely the last decade of the previous century, reveal no chronicle, almanac, magazine or work which refers to the alleged break. It also appears to be a general truth, common to all original sources, whatever their dates, that those who question Schikaneder's authorship never question the unity of the text, and vice versa. One is tempted to deduce from this that if one is intent upon attacking Schikaneder only one path can be chosen, for the choice of both would let Schikaneder off the hook.

On the more immediate scene neither Joachim Perinet nor Castelli referred to the break in the libretto, which does not mean that they were uncritical of Schikaneder. The latter openly chastised Schikaneder's grammatical and vocalic usage and Perinet, even in the midst of his eulogy in 1802, had most unkind things to say of Schikaneder's associations with the fair sex. Franz Gräffner's memoirs, published in 1845, no more distant from 1791 than Jahn's sources, indicate that Schikaneder wrote the libretto easily and quickly,[8] which would support Castelli's and Seyfried's view of his ready and fertile imagination,[9] and only offered it to Mozart after it had been completed. In general terms Nissen's decisive statement in his biography on Mozart's working methods upholds the same truth: "Es ist unmöglich, dass Mozart das Geringste von seiner dramatischen Musik erfunden, bevor der Charakter, die Situation und die Worte vor ihm standen."[10] Gräffner records even more intimate details of the association between Mozart and Schikaneder, revealing the latter as a forceful personality who not only demanded that Mozart's music should in certain instances appeal to the popular audience, but also provided him with the appropriate melodies. Clearly very knowledgeable about the creation of The Magic Flute, and most of Gräffner's assertions are confirmed elsewhere, he makes no reference to any remoulding of the text.

Motivation for the break was seen by Dent and Jahn to exist in the prior performance on June 8, 1791 of a popular comic opera Kaspar der Fagottist, in which the libretto was very similar in outline to that of *The Magic Flute*. Jahn's appraisal of the situation was that Schikaneder had been persuaded by the success of Giesecke's *Oberon, König der Elfen* in 1789, where the source had been acknowledged as Wieland, to turn to the same authority for material for his own magic opera. Jahn does not appear to have been aware that it was Schikaneder who commissioned Giesecke to write *Oberon* in the first place. Neither Schikaneder nor Perinet, the librettist of *Kaspar der Fagottist*, names a source for his text, but Jahn states that the latter's inspiration from *Lulu oder die Zauberflöte*, and the resulting performance of the opera on June 8 in the neighbouring Leopoldstadttheater, motivated Schikaneder's decision to alter the plot of *The Magic Flute*, as he, like Perinet, had had recourse to the original.[11] It has been explained in the previous chapter that it is perfectly feasible, indeed quite likely, that Schikaneder used one or two ideas from Liebeskind's fairy-tale. On the question of the break, however, the most important character of the opera becomes the Queen of Night and on this point, and absolutely consistently, Schikaneder's libretto is throughout completely different from both Perinet's opera and Liebeskind's fairy-tale. In this one aspect Perinet's libretto and Liebeskind's story are very similar, but again there are other distinctive features which differentiate between them. But where the good fairy in both the above versions takes the name "Perifirime, die strahlende Fee" and strikes her enemies blind by the intense light cast about her, Schikaneder's equivalent is quite explicitly a Queen of Night, representative of the forces of evil, superstition and darkness, and the greatest light which surrounds her is shed by the stars on her throne.

Jahn's conclusions have been founded apparently on textual parallels between the three plots in question, which indisputably exist. His hypothesis, however, has been confounded somewhat by truths of the kind uttered by Franz Grandaur, who, likewise comparing texts, deduces that Schikaneder availed himself of Terrasson's essay *Séthos*,[12] and by a wealth of material, some of it discussed previously, from the Old Viennese Popular Theatre. No evidence, other than that of textual parallels, which of course in an age of theatrical cliché and of popular traditions should not be given undue prominence, is of such a nature that it can state categorically that Schikaneder knew *Séthos* or *Lulu oder die*

Zauberflöte at first hand, yet Komorzynski has established beyond doubt that Schikaneder had a very intimate first-hand knowledge of Schiebeler's *Lisuart und Dariolette*. Again there is sufficient evidence to establish that Schikaneder was very well acquainted with the works of Hafner, and in particular his *Megära*, but none to show his knowledge of *Séthos* or *Lulu*. Still the latter two works and their similarities with *The Magic Flute* are not to be overlooked.

Mozart visited the Leopoldstadttheater three days after the first performance of *Kaspar der Fagottist*, on June 11, but could not recommend the opera. In his own words: "... ich ging dann um mich aufzuheitern zum Kasperl in die neue Oper der Fagottist, die so viel Lärm macht—aber gar nichts daran ist."[13]

The same letter, written on June 12 to Konstanze in Baden, refers in no way to the similarities between the two plots, which suggests that it was not uncommon in Vienna of the late eighteenth century for libretti to resemble each other. This can but give further support to the view that *The Magic Flute* arose not by a process of academic reference, but as the natural product of a tradition. It is, of course, reasonable to suggest that Mozart was at this time not yet occupied with writing the music to *The Magic Flute*, and hence, having no knowledge of the text, could not be expected to mention any similarities in his letter. Ironically, however, Jahn is one of the biographers who asserts that Schikaneder approached Mozart in the spring of 1791 to write the music for his libretto, and he further commits himself to a date, March 7. By July, according to the same authority, and also to Nissen, Mozart's work on the opera was far advanced.

The libretto of *The Magic Flute*, although there appear to be some minor inconsistencies, demonstrates in its main characters an overall unity. This is to be witnessed in particular in the development of the hero Tamino, whose outlook matures as the plot unfolds. Only unevenness in his character could confirm the view that the Queen of Night and Sarastro undergo a contrived change in theirs. By Act I, sc. xv Tamino has been established as an immature person and is here gently rebuked by the three genii for his youthful demeanour:

Dies kundzutun steht uns nicht an;
Sei standhaft, duldsam und verschwiegen.

Bedenke dies; kurz, sei ein Mann,
Dann, Jüngling, wirst du männlich siegen.[14]

The designation of the temples of Reason, Nature, and Wisdom, before which he now stands, is also instrumental in the portrayal of an immature prince. He casually equates Wisdom with Cleverness, and Reason and Nature with the Arts and Work,[15] revealing that as yet he has no true conception of the ideals upheld by the priesthood. With similar inference Tamino's attempt to enter the temple of Reason is impelled by only naïve considerations:

Ich wage mich mutig zur Pforte hinein,
Die Absicht ist edel und lauter und rein.
Erzittre, feiger Bösewicht!
Pamina retten, ist mir Pflicht.[16]

He is therefore severely warned about desecrating the temple. Tamino then decides to try his luck at the temple of Nature and entry is once again refused. Summoned by a modest knock at the door of the temple of Wisdom, a priest now confronts him and acknowledges only the prince's youthful and courageous qualities. When Tamino declares that he is seeking the "possession of love and virtue", the priest becomes almost disdainful in his reply:

Die Worte sind von hohem Sinne!
Allein wie willst du diese finden?
Dich leitet Lieb' und Tugend nicht,
Weil Tod und Rache dich entzünden.[17]

The desire for "death and revenge" condemns Tamino now as it later condemns the Queen of Night. Upon discovering that Sarastro, to him an evil power, rules in the temple of Wisdom he is shocked by the hypocrisy of the situation, and although his subsequent decision not to see the temple reveals some inborn virtue, it prompts him to forget completely the purpose of his mission, the rescue of Pamina. On the point of forsaking his beloved, Tamino is restrained by the priest, who sees that the prince has been deceived:

Erklär dich näher mir,
Dich täuschet ein Betrug.[18]

Hitherto Tamino has understood the Queen of Night and her three ladies to be manifestations of a good power and he is now asked how he came by his bad opinion of Sarastro. His gullible nature is underlined by his own explanation and the priest's commentary:

PRIESTER:
   ... Sarastro hassest du?

TAMINO:
   Ich hass' ihn ewig! ja!

PRIESTER:
   Nun gib mir deine Gründe an.

TAMINO:
   Er ist ein Unmensch, ein Tyrann.

PRIESTER:
   Ist das, was du gesagt, erwiesen?

TAMINO:
   Durch ein unglücklich Weib bewiesen,
   Das Gram und Jammer niederdrückt.

PRIESTER:
   Ein Weib hat also dich berückt?
   Ein Weib tut wenig, plaudert viel.
   Du, Jüngling, glaubst dem Zungenspiel?
   O legte doch Sarastro dir
   Die Absicht seiner Handlung für.[19]

The priest is clearly convinced of Sarastro's good motives for abducting Pamina, as he acknowledges the truth of Tamino's accusation, but it is inferred that in his present state of mind the prince could not understand them. The laws which govern the priest will not allow him to state Sarastro's reasons, or to inform Tamino whether Pamina is dead or alive. The prince's main concern for the moment is in fact this latter question and yet he is already beginning to express a longing for knowledge which extends beyond the realm of personal interest. As soon as he discovers that initiation into the priesthood will remove his delusion, Tamino longs to be enlightened:

O ewige Nacht, wann wirst du schwinden?
Wann wird das Licht mein Auge finden?[20]

Night as the symbol of ignorance and superstition is a theme which transcends the merely metaphorical use which is placed upon it here. Later in Act II, Sc. i Sarastro himself refers to the "nightly veil" which Tamino must tear from his eyes if he wishes to perceive the "great light" of the priesthood.

Act I, Sc. xv is vital as the pivot around which the plot revolves. The Viennese theatre almanac of 1804, which, referring to a performance of the opera in Leipzig in 1803, criticizes the almost inaudible singing of the three genii and comments that the *Maschinerie* was so quick that the thunder preceded the lightning, remarks also on the effects of omitting three pages from the libretto, clearly an omission from this very scene:

Die Plötzliche Verwandlung
Warum wurde so schnell hier Rache in Freundschaft verwandelt?
Weil—so spricht der Souffleur, weil man drey Seiten vergass.[21]

In this instance not only Tamino's change of attitude would have appeared unmotivated, but it must have been impossible to believe in the presentation of the Queen of Night as an evil power and of Sarastro as a good power in the following scenes.

In further support of the libretto's overall unity it appears that Mozart recognized the evil in the Queen's character from the beginning of the opera. Both her arias, the one in the first act before the alleged "break" and the second in Act II, are proud and demonic, although a degree of compassion is to be noted in the recitative of the first. Such an appraisal of the Queen of Night is also substantiated by Mozart's intentional use of Italian bravura where it is almost completely lacking in the other musical parts of the opera. Mozart and Schikaneder in Vienna and on the strolling and court stages suffered alike from the national preference for the theatrical art of France and Italy and were conscious of the need to establish Germany as a cultural force.[22] In 1777 C. F. Weisse noted with some consternation that even the naïvely conceived and musically unpretentious German *Singspiel* was in danger of being burdened with the artificial brilliance of Italian coloratura.[23] In the late eighteenth century the same style was applied in Vienna with great success by a Spaniard, Vicenz Martín y Soler, who had acquired his technique from Italy. In his novel *Mozart auf der Reise nach Prag* (1856), Mörike infers that Soler's unmerited popularity was even resented by Mozart,[24] while, according to Cornet's *Die Oper in Deutschland*, Madame Mozart later confessed that in the musical rôle of the Queen of Night her husband had deliberately satirized such aesthetically insincere practices.[25] Nissen's comments on the musical nature of the Queen of Night also reveal how deliberate Mozart was in his approach in this matter:

> ... Die Höhe der Königin der Nacht ist ein Probierstein für hohe Kopfstimmen; denn melodischen Gesang und sanftes Tragen der Töne fand Mozarts Weisheit dieser racheschnaubenden Königin zu ertheilen nicht für gut.[26]

It would therefore appear to be established that Mozart perceived from the outset the hypocritical and evil nature of the Queen and took advantage of her situation in the opera to express his own dissatisfaction with both popular and Imperial attitudes in Vienna to Italian music, the very nature of which as Mozart declared in his letters, limited the sincerity of its appeal. No doubt also Madame Hofer, Mozart's sister-in-law and the leading soprano of Schikaneder's theatre who took the part of the Queen of Night, had not a little influence on the forming of the character of the Queen of Night. With regard to her nature Mozart describes her in the most disparaging terms as "eine faule, grobe Person, die es dick hinter den Ohren hat".[27] Musically she was quite gifted but Castelli takes the trouble to point out that the nature of her gifts was that of a "Bravoursängerin", who excelled in staccato singing in the high register. When Bauernfeld was still co-director of the Leopoldstadttheater in 1790,[28] he and Schikaneder had signed a contract with Madame Hofer and when this agreement is viewed together with Schikaneder's long established habit of writing plays and libretti tailored to suit the various talents of the individual members of his company, it becomes clear that Madame Hofer herself had some considerable influence on the shaping of the character of the Queen of Night. It is also to be noted that she later in 1796 took the part of Frau von Tiefsinn in Schikaneder's very successful popular comic opera *Der Tyroler Wastel* and that the characters, but not the rôles, of Frau von Tiefsinn and the Queen of Night are very similar indeed.[29]

It is self-evident that the libretto formed the basis of Mozart's understanding of the character of the Queen of Night. Her rôle is dual but not contradictory. On the human plane she is drawn as a widow who dotes on her only child, Pamina, and when her daughter is abducted, she is seen as an overwrought mother, whose deprivation forces her to behave in a malicious way in the attempt to regain her "property" and have her wishes fulfilled. As a Queen she is the symbol of all the qualities of night, of its darkness, its magic, its superstition, its evil and hypocrisy, elements which inevitably colour her humanity. Even in the words of the first aria, before the fictitious break, the true cause of her distress at the loss of her daughter to Sarastro clearly consists of pity for her own plight rather than of genuine con-concern for her daughter's safety. The aria fails to mention what torture might be inflicted on Pamina, which reveals the Queen as either a callous and unimaginative mother, or as one who knows that Sarastro is not an evil power. That such a depiction of insincerity was intended is further supported by its earlier appearance in the popular works of C. F. Weisse and Philipp Hafner, revealing itself as part of the wider traditional inheritance of the opera.

The Queen's dislike of Sarastro is a constant and consistent theme of the libretto, as is the latter's opinion of her as a proud woman. When in 1794 C. V. Vulpius attempted, incidentally without success, to give an improved version of the libretto of *The Magic Flute*, he stated that one of the main faults he had to find with the original libretto was that the rhyming was bad. However, the Vulpius version did not improve the rhyming, but instead altered very slightly the shades of meaning in various parts of the opera. Thus in the case of the Queen of Night and Sarastro's opinion of her the epithet "proud" is replaced by "evil"[30] This, as with all other changes by Vulpius, tends to make clearer the distinctions between black and white, between evil and good, where Schikaneder clearly intended those same distinctions to be made visually by the stage production. In Schikaneder's original it is pride which cannot allow the Queen's deceased husband's power, with the exception of "der siebenfache Sonnenkreis" over which she has no control, to pass into the hands of its proper heir, Sarastro. That her authority is usurped is seen as the Queen's political transgression and for this and her hypocrisy she is condemned at the end of the opera:

Die Strahlen der Sonne vertreiben die Nacht,
Zernichten der Heuchler erschlichene Nacht.[31]

In addition to her personal and political failings the Queen is also guilty of the neglect of maternal duty, an attitude which provides the motive for Sarastro's abduction of Pamina. He sees in the Queen of Night an influence which would be harmful to Pamina and he is therefore obliged to act according to the revelations of his omniscience. When Pamina tries to escape she flees before the evil advances of Monostatos, not from Sarastro, whom she acknowledges as a good power throughout. Later in the opera the evil in the Queen overrides any maternal instincts, with which she may have been accredited, when she imposes upon her daughter the task of stabbing Sarastro to death. Significantly it is now Pamina's turn to doubt the conception of her mother as a good person, and it is after all quite natural that her enlightenment in this matter should not proceed as quickly as Tamino's. Clearly Pamina's isolation from her mother's influence has in the meantime helped her to this degree of objective appraisal. Pamina cannot find it in her to murder Sarastro, although on the other hand she is only gradually convinced that he is representative of a good power. When the evil of Monostatos is discovered as he is about to kill Pamina, Sarastro's condemnation of the Queen of Night recurs once more and charitably tempers his judgement of the Negro slave:

Ich weiss nur allzuviel—weiss, dass deine Seele ebenso schwarz als dein Gesicht ist. Auch würde ich dies schwarze Unternehmen mit höchster Strenge an dir bestrafen, wenn nicht ein böses Weib, das zwar eine sehr gute Tochter hat, den Dolch dazu geschmiedet hätte. Verdank' es der bösen Handlung des Weibes, dass du ungestraft davonziehst. Geh![32]

The human, and in particular, the maternal aspect of the Queen of Night, as a result of her abuse of these instincts, diminishes wholly yet almost imperceptibly, until she is finally banished by Sarastro in the only rôle remaining to her as the symbol of darkness and evil.

An examination of the libretto prior to the supposed break, centring on the two main characters at this stage, the Queen and Tamino, tends to uphold the unity of the text, although Brigid Brophy has seen here only irreconcilable elements. She would exclude any moral subtlety from the Viennese popular theatre and can therefore accept only the obvious interpretation of the opening scene of the opera, in which the serpent is killed by the three Ladies of the Queen of Night and Tamino's life is subsequently saved. The conclusion drawn is, of course, that this is the act of a good power. Unfortunately such a hypothesis rests on the wrong assumption that the Viennese audience had never before witnessed a plot of this kind and would consequently require the representation of the moral issues to be clear and obvious.[33] On the one hand the audience was in fact very intimately acquainted with plots similar to that of *The Magic Flute*, as previous chapters have shown, and on the other, popular theatre by 1791 had in any case departed from its original naïvety, particularly in Schikaneder's theatre, although it had remained truer to its unpretentious origins in Marinelli's Kasperl-theater. Moral subtleties were already to be found in Hafner's works in the 60's. The libretto provides an alternative answer to the obvious one.

The opera has associations with ancient Egypt and with the Orient and both worlds exerted an influence on the popular theatre of Vienna. The theatre's indebtedness to the legendry of Wieland and to that of a Thousand and One Nights[34] is indisputable, so that it is not surprising to find the presence of the serpent in *The Magic Flute* justified and explained by an Eastern myth, which reported the common Indian belief that a wealthy man who died without heir would return to guard his wealth in the form of a serpent. No details have arisen to prove beyond doubt that this was in Schikaneder's mind, but it is remarkable how exactly the belief is reproduced in Schikaneder's libretto. The Queen's late husband was wealthy and powerful, he died without heir as he had no son, only a daughter, Pamina, and he therefore, so it may be deduced, returns in the form of a serpent to guard his wealth. When Tamino enters it is evident from his "japanisches Jagdkleid", an attribute of which Vulpius declares that he can make no sense, and which he therefore alters in his version of the text, that he is a trespasser on foreign soil. Because of this he is attacked by the serpent. The three Ladies, representatives of the Queen, who has usurped the serpent's kingdom, kill the serpent, which act frees both them and the treasure, including incidentally the magic flute and bells, from its guardianship. In so doing they save Tamino, who, gullible and immature, imagines that these forces of "evil" sought his salvation alone, where instead it may be deduced that they took advantage of the peculiar situation of the serpent to destroy it. In the way of popular humour the three Ladies are, moreover, chastised for their rather selfish attitude towards the handsome prince, an attitude which is not easily reconciled with a good power.

Despite all that may be levied against Vulpius's version of Schikaneder's text, it is interesting to try and deduce the thinking behind Vulpius's changes. For instance, Vulpius clearly fails to realize why it is important to have a serpent chase Tamino, and not, as in his version, a "fire-breathing dragon", which incidentally Vulpius does not have killed, but merely chased back into its cave. The reasons behind this change are given by Vulpius in the preface and are reasons entirely unrelated to an interpretation of the text. Quite obviously Vulpius is not referring to any production by Schikaneder, for as a producer and theatrical craftsman Schikaneder's genius has been indisputably established, when he complains that more often than not the serpent does not even arrive on stage, because the technical apparatus fails, and the three Ladies find themselves in the embarrassing situation of having "to throttle to death the boards of the stage".[35] Clearly Vulpius had little knowledge of the real, practical genius of Schikaneder. This lack in him also appears to underline a further point about his version of the libretto, for he clumsily makes a point of adding even greater emphasis to the fact that the Queen's power is usurped. Papageno becomes a painfully obvious expositeur in the early scenes and is given an entirely new speech by Vulpius. The speech contains no new information about the Queen's situation, but it gives that information much earlier than Schikaneder did:

Je nun! Du weisst doch wohl, dass Sarastros Bruder, der Gemahl der Königin der Nacht war? dass er starb, und nur eine Tochter aber keinen Sohn hinterliess? dass das Reich einen *männlichen* Regenten fordert? dass ein Weib hier nicht regieren kann? dass also Sarastro seinem Bruder in der Regierung folgte? und dass die Königin der Nacht, ausser ihrem Witthume, dem Reiche, der Nacht (*vor sich*) O! ich Einfaltspinsel! (*Pfeift*).[36]

It is for this information that Papageno is punished by the imposition of the lock. Clearly Vulpius thought that here was a feature about the libretto which was insufficiently explained and he saw to it that his own version clarified matters, which undoubtedly it did. It neglected, however, to realize that Schikaneder's theatre was a baroque theatre, which meant per se that its attraction was not a literary one, but a textual *and* visual one. This can be proved on two other occasions. In his preface Vulpius criticizes the libretto from the standpoint of one who does not know that Schikaneder's theatre is traditionally baroque and popular, for he questions it as one would question the literary theatre and the French classical drama of the day: "Das Originalstück hat gar keinen Plan. Die Menschen gehen darinne nur, um wieder zu kommen, und kommen, um abgehen zu können. . ."[37] Similarly, Vulpius explains his reasons for giving his version three acts, where Schikaneder's version had only two. The change, apparently, was motivated by the consideration that Act II of Schikaneder's original was inordinately long. The effect of this, of course, was to entirely upset the symmetry of the visual presentation of the opera, for Act I was intended by Schikaneder to occur with Tamino as yet a victim of his own spiritual darkness and Act II, which significantly was accompanied by stage directions to emphasize the gradual dawning of physical light, was to realize Tamino's spiritual enlightenment by a process of ordeal and initiation into the priesthood. Clearly Vulpius did not account sufficiently for Schikaneder's theatrical interpretation of the text.

But even in Schikaneder's original, Papageno infers that the Queen is something of a tyrant, despite the fact that he himself is in her service. In several ways it is illustrated how much his freedom is restricted: he is delighted to discover that other mountains, people and countries exist; he had been informed that his mother had served the Queen in a building which was locked, possibly referring to his cage; he describes the Queen as an awesome and remote authority, where on the other hand Sarastro is more readily approachable, and does so in such a way as to inspire fear of her, and, finally, he lives on food and drink which are given to him daily in exchange for the birds he catches for the Queen and her attendants.[38]

Whatever reasons may be given for supposing the three Ladies to be servants of a good power and therefore good themselves, tend to lose their validity when the method by which they ensnare Tamino is considered. From the beginning their visual aspect is awesome, they are veiled and carry silver javelins. The presence of the veils is to Papageno proof that the three Ladies are ugly, and, ironically, he calls them "meine Schönen". The as yet immature Tamino assumes, however, that the faces behind the veils are beautiful, but Papageno contradicts him on this point, acting in his traditional rôle as "Sittenlehrer" to the hero. Vulpius again sees it his duty to clarify the situation merely in terms of the libretto:

> PAPAGENO: Glaub' mir! die Schleiertrachten taugen zu gar nichts, als dazu, einen ehrlichen Kerl hinter's Licht zu führen.
>
> DIE DREI DAMEN (*drohend*): Papageno!
>
> PAPAGENO: Sie nehmen's übel! Die Frauenzimmer hören nie gern die Wahrheit, wenn sie ihre Reitze betrift. (*Zu den Damen.*)[39]

For his failings Papageno is later chastised by Sarastro, but is nevertheless treated with some benignity as the latter's omniscience acknowledges that the popular comedian in Papageno is incorrigible. However, for his pretence of heroism in Act I Sc. ii Papageno is punished by the three Ladies who give him water instead of wine, stone instead of sugar-bread, and put a golden padlock on his mouth. The Queen thus imposes silence physically on Papageno, whereas later under Sarastro's auspices he is asked to observe silence voluntarily, if he wishes to be admitted to the priesthood. The imposition of the lock is, however, no mere theatrical trick, as might be supposed, but serves, so it might be deduced, an additional purpose, one which Vulpius appears to acknowledge. It would not in the circumstances be the Queen's wish that Tamino should be grateful to Papageno for having saved his life: he must be grateful to her servants, the three Ladies, so that together indebtedness and love for Pamina can ensnare him inextricably.

The sequence of events thus becomes important, where Tamino is first presented with a portrait of the Queen's daughter, he then reacts by falling in love with it—a meaningless incident morally speaking, which was used by Hafner in 1763 to demonstrate affectation rather than affection—and finally, not until after Tamino's complete surrender to his feelings in the aria "Dies Bildnis ist bezaubernd schön . . .", is he supplied with the information that Pamina is for the moment unattainable. In his subsequent despair the immature Tamino readily believes that Sarastro is, as the three Ladies take care to inform him, "ein mächtiger böser Dämon". Yet even they admit that Sarastro lives in pleasant surroundings. Nissen's biography of Mozart was explicit in indicating the guile and subtlety of the Queen's approach to Tamino:

> Fliesst nicht im Gesange des Sarastro und in den Chören der Priester die reinste Sprache tiefer, von aller Leidenschaft abgetrennter Weisheit? Man kann sich nicht täuschen: nur eine beruhigte Welt von Eingeweihten singt solche Töne. Hört man dagegen die Königin der Nacht, zur Hälfte schon im Gesange ihrer verschleierten Damen gezeichnet; prächtig und stolz beginnt ihr Gesang, lockend gegen den Jüngling, den sie zu gewinnen strebt, und mit dem Flittergolde weiblicher Eitelkeit besetzt. Racheglühend, von allen finstern Leidenschaften aufgewühlt, als Mutter und Königin gebietend erscheint die Beherrscherin der Nacht in der zweyten Arie. Nur eine sternflammende Königin kann diese Arie singen. . .[40]

The Queen retains her awesomeness when she appears before Tamino, which, of course, does not commit her to goodness or evil. As she enlists the prince's help in the rescue of her daughter, she confesses that she did not have the power to keep Pamina safe from Sarastro, an admission which is better understood later when it is discovered that Sarastro possesses the ultimate weapon "der siebenfachen Sonnenkreis". At this point in the plot the Queen of Night does not reveal her political motives. For her, Tamino's being provides a kind of magic recipe for the recovery of the princess. In particular, the use of the adverb "am besten" suggests that in her eyes Tamino's qualities of being "unschuldig, weise, fromm" are the exact prescription for this particular situation. Indeed it is soon revealed that these same qualities will enable Tamino to enter the priesthood and in so doing gain his Pamina. In her first aria the Queen's implication is that Tamino is the type needed to appeal to Sarastro. She schemes here as she does later with her own daughter in the attempt to murder Sarastro. Further upholding the hypocrisy of her situation, she has entered the plot as a magical apparition, where Sarastro is embodied as a reality.

The theme of revenge is an integral part of the moral concern of the plot and is inevitably linked with the rôles of the three main participants, the Queen of Night, Sarastro and Tamino. A correct understanding of the application of the passion of revenge within the plots leads also to a revelation of the plot's inherent unity. The desire for revenge which motivates Tamino's adventure initially and with which he encounters the priest, is condemned by the latter straightway, and the gentle and charitable nature of the priesthood in general is further embodied in Sarastro's aria, "In diesen heil'gen Hallen kennt man die Rache nicht. . ." The spirit behind Sarastro's government is one of tolerance and charity, yet he does administer punishment—as in the case of Monostato's unenlightened transgression where he attempted to force his advances upon Pamina—and he finally banishes the Queen of Night from the presence of Light. Vulpius's version fails to distinguish however, between what the Queen sees as justice and what Sarastro sees as justice, for he replaces Schikaneder's description of Sarastro as "der göttliche Weise" (The divinely Wise) with "der strafende Rächer" (the punishing Avenger), which, of course, would make him, the king of wisdom, as guilty and as intolerant as Tamino and the Queen of Night, and blur the otherwise clear distinctions between Sarastro and the Queen.

The rôle of the three genii also requires some explanation in order to establish the unity of their function. Quite commonly the criticism is raised that the genii first appear to owe allegiance to the Queen and then later give their undivided support to Sarastro's cause. Such criticism, however unenlightened it may be, unfortunately has been further manipulated to prove the existence of a break in the libretto. The article on *The Magic Flute* in the *Monatschrift für Theater und Musik* of 1857 voices the same criticism, but the author himself exposes the weakness of his argument:

> . . . wo sie (3 Damen) ihn (Tamino) auf die drei zarten Knäblein hinweisen, die seine Führer sein sollen, folglich im Dienste der Königin stehen, während sie im weiteren Verlaufe der Oper Geschöpfe Sarastros und Taminos und Paminas Schützer gegen die schwarzen Pläne der Königin werden. . .[41]

He clearly jumps to the conclusion, a fairly obvious one admittedly, that the genii are therefore in the service of the Queen. It is, however, nowhere stated in Schikaneder's libretto that the genii serve either the Queen of Night or Sarastro. This approach now gives added unity to the text for in this light the genii appear as those supernatural powers, subservient to no-one, who guide the good, if immature, Tamino, along the right path. Their function is therefore necessarily vague, similar to the good fairies of the opera. The story of *Die klugen Knaben*, of which there are three, which appeared in the third volume of *Dschinnistan* in 1789,[42] gives the three genii exactly this rôle, so that they do not serve, but only exist to be consulted in an advisory capacity, and thus give guidance to those who require it. But they are clearly a good force and are guilty of no act for the cause of evil.

NOTES

Chapter 1

THE OLD VIENNESE POPULAR THEATRE

1. *Die Alt-Wiener Volkskomödie*, O. Rommel, Vienna, 1952, p. 171.
2. *Geschichte der deutschen Schauspielkunst*, E. Devrient, Berlin, 1905, I, 99.
3. Rommel, op. cit., p. 187.
   It's my job, for good or for ill, to discharge the offices given me, to be stupid one moment and witty the next, to cudgel and be cudgelled, to deceive one and do another a favour, to act the lover, the glutton, the loafer or the drunkard.
4. Rommel gives convincing evidence to show that Stranitzky died in 1726 at the age of fifty. However the Vienna theatre almanac of 1804 reports that Stranitzky died in 1727 after having engaged Schröter and Leinhaas in the same year. (p. 89ff.) The Gotha theatre calendar of 1776 confirms the latter source with the date 1727. (p. 148.)
5. *Das Schauspiel der Wanderbühne*, W. Flemming, Reihe Barock, Leipzig, 1931, III, 7.
6. Devrient, op. cit., VIII, 184ff.
   Gotha Theaterkalender, 1776, p. 119.
7. *Alt-Wiener Theaterlieder*, Vienna and Berlin, 1920, p. XIf.
   Hans Wurst came on stage wearing a tall green pointed hat, his hair was fastened up so that it came to a point, his thick eyebrows were heavily drawn and came together over his nose. His beard too was pointed and he had a small moustache without an imperial, so that his expressive mouth remained clearly visible. Around his neck he wore a large, white ruff. His short jacket, which had long, narrow sleeves, boasted a green patch at the front where a large heart was to be seen with the embroidered letters H W, the trousers were long and fastened round the ankles at the bottom, from his back hung the fat, sausage-like bag, which gave Hans Wurst his name, at his side he had a wooden sword and on his feet he wore the strapped clogs of the peasant. The most characteristic thing about him, to which the plays refer repeatedly, was probably the patch on his coat. Asked whether he had a heart, he would respond with: "Of course I have, on my patch".

8. *Die Maschinenkomödie,* Barocktradition 1. (hereinafter referred to as M. Bt. 1) ed. O. Rommel, Leipzig, 1935, p. 23.

    The river Tiber, its banks made attractive by a beautiful garden and shady trees, enter Julius Antonius, Lucio Scipio and Hans Wurst on gondolas.

9. Rommel, op. cit., p. 230.

10. Smekal, op. cit., p. Xf.

11. *Ollapatrida des durchgetriebenen Fuchsmundi,* J. Stranitzky, Vienna, 1711, 3, 20ff.

    When the devil heard the conjuration and that he was going to cause his evil wife to appear, he was so afraid that he begged forgiveness from both Heaven and Hell. Not only did he obediently leave at once, but gave all the money he had previously gained to the herbalist, provided he would keep his evil wife away. So you see, Sir, even the devil is afraid of a wicked woman.

12. ibid., 7, 48ff.

    Truly I have quite a fat backside, but my doctor has promised me that he'll get rid of it, and with goat's whey. . . He assures me that it's only certain "acres of humours" which spread through the diaphragm and mensentarium and then fall down into my seat.

13. ibid., 1, 4ff.

    MASTER: Why shouldn't I fall in love like you?

    FUCHSMUNDI: Like me? Well if you do as I do, you certainly wouldn't be so scraggy and fret with impatience. Even when I'm in love, I see to it that it's doing me some good at least. When I've a glass of wine of a fresh, sparkling hue before me, and a well-proportioned pheasant with a superb breast, I immediately forget all other twaddle and don't give a thought to Isabella or Rosalia or any other such rot, for it only stirs you up inside.

    MASTER: Have you quite finished?

    FUCHSMUNDI: That's merely the introduction, I haven't even begun yet. . .

14. ibid.

    FUCHSMUNDI: My lord, you should keep out of this marriage, unless you wish to join the great world brotherhood Fratrum Corneliorum. Here, admittedly, you would be crowned, but by others you would be ridiculed. In this day and age there's nothing at all to commend such great stags, who play their part in conforming to the usual way of the world. Love now is so very dangerous that he who succumbs would speak thus:
    Even though it displeases me,
    You people can give it me in writing
    That I'm an arch-fantast.
    Of necessity you force me to confess
    At last before all the world

This foolishness of mine.
I can hear nothing with my ears,
The eyes which saw, are blind,
My mouth has lost its taste.
My fists know not why nor wherefore,
My nose smells and straightway
Gets the sniffs, when it should by rights be smelling.
There's a rafter missing from my skull,
My head is like a dove-cote,
Young fools are flying
In at the front and out at the back.
But in the evening they re-assemble here
In their quarters.
Unless you can build me a hide,
Where I can lock myself away,
Set upon me the children on the street
With their cats and dogs,
And call me all the names you will
Until I cease to act so foolishly.
Singe my head with blows,
And fix in me a fox's tail.
If you wish to order me a hat,
Then stitch a dunce's cap thereto,
And give me not a sabre,
But a wooden sword which has no sheath,
Set my clothes with coloured patches
And make me a ribbon of bean straw,
Write of me in all corners,
This is a fool in folio.
But for this fool's game
I desire not recognition.

15. ibid., 4, 27ff.

16. Smekal, op. cit., p. XII.

17. p. 89ff.

18. *Hafners Gesammelte Schriften*, 3 vol., Vienna, 1812.

19. p. 83ff.

20. ibid., p. 81.
    All the improvised plays had a framework which could be very
    meagre as the actors knew exactly where best their various comic
    talents lay and were so used to each other, which was the only
    way possible of achieving the so-called ensemble, a completely, if
    I may use the term, round performance.

21. Rommel, op. cit., p. 338ff.
    Wiener Hoftheateralmanach, 1804 (hereinafter referred to as WHTA),
    p. 89ff.

22. cf., Smekal, op. cit., p. XV.
> HANS WURST:
>> Colombine, little mouse!
>> More beautiful than a bunch of wall-flowers!
> COLOMBINE:
>> Little sausage, dearest heart,
>> More tender than spinach and rump.
> HANS WURST:
>> Whiter than chalk and snow!
> COLOMBINE:
>> Milder than medicinal tea!

23. M. Bt. 1. p. 77ff.
>> O you poor world!
>> Are you not aware
>> That each moment is shortening our life.
>> O you poor world!
>> And now you are bent on
>> Deceiving your neighbour
>> With words and with lying,
>> Envying his fortune,
>> Curtailing his honour,
>>> Now singing,
>>> And jumping,
>> Now quoffing and gorging,
>> Now playing and dancing,
>>> Now Styrian,
>>> And Swabian,
>>> Hanakian,
>>> Slovakian,
>> Now walzing umatum,
>> He sa rum rum,
>>> O you poor world,
>>> Now what a plight you're in.

24. ibid, p. 81-83. (*The recharged and revitalized Bernardon.*)
> ISABELLA:
>> I feel in my heart a hell-fire burning,
>> I'm nigh bursting with anger, revenge and with rage, (to Hans Wurst).
>> Come here and devour me thou horrible monster.
> HANS WURST (*fearfully*):
>> Oh, if only I were away from here,
>> It would be all right by me,
>> Madam, I'm the bridegroom.
> ISABELLA (*kindly*):
>> Yes, yes, I know thee,
>> Thou art the one who took my heart, (*they embrace*).
>> O come!

HANS WURST:
Here I am.
ISABELLA (*in a rage she thrusts Hans Wurst from her*):
Away thou basilisque, away thou crocodile,
Thou thirstest for blood alone.
HANS WURST:
On my word, that's going too far,
I'm the Hans Wurst.
ISABELLA (*kindly*):
My angel, come, embrace me.
HANS WURST (*fearfully, embraces her*):
I wonder what now?
ISABELLA (*with a dagger*):
Die murderer, I have thee, thou rogue.
HANS WURST (*anxiously*):
Alas! Woe is me!
ISABELLA:
Willt thou love?
HANS WURST:
Yes.
ISABELLA:
Willt thou die?
HANS WURST:
No.
ISABELLA:
Willt thou love?
HANS WURST:
Yes.
ISABELLA:
Willt thou die?
HANS WURST:
No.
ISABELLA:
Willt thou die?
HANS WURST:
No.
ISABELLA:
Willt thou love?
HANS WURST:
Yes.
ISABELLA:
Willt thou love?
HANS WURST:
Yes.
ISABELLA:
Willt thou die?
HANS WURST:
No.

ISABELLA:
Right, thou shalt love.
HANS WURST:
Would that I'd stayed at home.
ISABELLA (*solemnly*):
Hear my resolve:
In the very midst of torment, thou shallt ever remain with me,
In sorrow, fear and poverty,
Shallt thou spend the whole of thy life with me,
Hard upon it death will follow,
Let our union be torment and suffering.
HANS WURST (*adagio*):
O what a marvellous marriage!
ISABELLA (*joyfully*):
Come, my life! Come, my heart!
Come to the wedding and be of good cheer.
HANS WURST:
I'd rather go right away
To the mad-house in St. Marx.
(*Isabella takes Hans Wurst by the hand and exits with him, jumping around, trara, trara.*)

25. ibid., p. 106.
ALL:
Alas! We're all lost,
The devil is afoot,
I know not where I am,
I'm much too afraid.
(*Fiametta appears as a ghost.*)
FIAMETTA:
I am the ghost of Fiametta,
Who delivers you your punishment.
(*Bernardon also appears as a ghost.*)
BERNARDON:
And I am Bernardon,
Who gives you your reward.

26. *Die Musik in der Wiener deutschen Stegreifkomödie*, R. Haas (Vienna, 1925), p. 54f.

27. Smekal, op. cit., p. XVI.

28. *Comedy in Germany in the first half of the eighteenth Century*, B. Aitken-Sneath, p. 42.

29. M. Bt. 1.

30. *Emanuel Schikaneder*, E. Komorzynski, Wiesbaden and Vienna, 1951.

Chapter 2

THE CONFLICT BETWEEN OLD VIENNESE POPULAR THEATRE AND LITERARY DRAMA IN THE KÄRNTNERTHORTHEATER

1. WHTA, p. 89ff.
2. Sellier had engaged Heydrich, Lorenzin, Koch and his wife from Karoline Neuber's company of strolling players.
   Rommel, op. cit., p. 382.
   WHTA, p. 89ff.
3. ibid.
   They produced Alzire, pretending that they themselves were there to perform in these plays . . . Madam Nuth, a woman of 46 with an ungainly body, played the part of Alzire; Madam Schröter and Madam Müller, each of them more than 40 years old, were her two confidantes, Huber played Zamor, Schröter played Alvar and Mayberg, Montez. They cut whatever they wanted, to save themselves the trouble of learning their parts, in a word, the play was hashed completely.
4. ibid.
   The Comedy shall perform no compositions other than those which come from the French, Italian or Spanish theatres. All local plays by Bernardon and others shall be stopped forthwith, but if there are any good ones by Weiskern, they shall be read first, no equivocal or dirty words shall be allowed in them, nor shall any of the actors use the same without due punishment.
5. p. 26.
   . . . and of which the censor saw it necessary to suppress some verses in order to defend the public from any unpleasantness. But why did the comic sing on the stage, in public, what was not allowed to be printed?
6. WHTA, p. 89ff.
   "Through this the native drama appeared greatly inferior to the foreign one, and the neatness, pomp and meticulous order which prevailed at the French performances could only serve to discredit the German actors in the eyes of the public."
7. cf., p. 58ff.
8. *Gotha Theaterkalender,* 1776:
   Dramatischer Antikritikus von Wien, H. Borgers, 1775.
   Genaue Nachrichten von beyden k.k. Schaubühnen und andern öffentlichen Ergötzlichkeiten in Wien, H. Müller, Pressburg, 1772 & 1773.
   Theaterchronik von Wien, H. von Moll, 1774.
   Über die deutsche komische Oper, H. Reichhardt, Hamburg, 1775.

Wiener Allerley, eine Monatschrift, Vienna, 1774.
Wienerische Dramaturgie, Vienna, 1775.
Der Zeigefinger, eine Wochenschrift, Vienna, 1774.

9. See under: *Verzeichniss aller lebenden deutschen Schriftsteller die für das Theater gearbeitet haben.*

10. WHTA, p. 89ff.
". . . French comedy, which had always been its favourite form of drama."

11. ibid.
Without any knowledge of the German language, or determination or skill in the handling of the theatre, Afflisio let himself be led blindly by those who advised him to present only farces if he wished to draw some profit from the undertaking. He followed this advice faithfully, neglected the national theatre completely and spent large sums of money on the French theatre, the opera buffa and ballet.

12. cf., note 8.

13. WHTA, p. 89ff.
". . . refused permission to all other companies to play at the Royal Imperial Theatre and extemporized acting was forbidden."

14. Böhm's strolling company was playing in Salzburg when the Mozart family was there in 1779. When his company left after some success, it was succeeded by Schikaneder's company which arrived in September, 1780. Both Böhm and Schikaneder had had considerable success by this time with the performance of *Singspiel.*

15. p. 78.
Original plays for the German nation, works of true genius, where nature and art are properly allied and whose authors neither ignore the rules nor allow themselves to be inhibited in their flights of poetic fancy by any arbitrary prescription. Plays of this kind are still few in number and it is the wish of all friends of the German National Theatre to see them multiplied.

The management of the Royal Imperial Theatre will by this public notice seek to encourage all those intellects in Germany, who are capable of responding, to help in spreading the fame of the national stage; and if they care to produce for Vienna good and useful original plays, they shall receive the following in payment:

For an unprinted play of usual length, complete plays, whether they be tragedies or comedies, they shall receive paid to them on the following day without any reduction the theatre's takings on the evening of the third performance. Smaller plays of value can be estimated at half the rate mentioned above. One thing we should like to point out, especially to writers from outside Vienna, who send their works to us, is that they should continually bear in mind our audience in Vienna, this locality and the present age. Whatever general observations may be made in addition would seem superfluous here.

Every author can moreover rest assured that the acceptance or rejection of his play will not be determined by overindulgent criticism, but only in consideration of our theatre and our audience; also that the Royal Imperial Censor is accustomed to exercising his authority in this matter.

Manuscripts can be forwarded to Stephanie the elder, producer to the National Theatre, who after the passing of one month, reckoning from the day of receipt, will either accept or return the manuscript. . .

16. ibid.

17. The almanac notes the decree:
". . . that furthermore no additional freedom should be automatically allowed, rather would every native and foreign strolling company of actors be free to occupy the Kärntnerthortheater, and to give plays at their own risk. . ."

18. Komorzynski, op. cit.
The Revolutionary Emperor, S. K. Padover, London, 1934, p. 106ff.

Chapter 3

PHILIPP HAFNER AND THE GROWTH OF POPULAR VIENNESE TRADITIONS

1. I, VI.
The man who was responsible for writing materials at the City Court was very niggardly with paper. Hafner was to take the first hearing of a person who had been brought to court. He sent for some paper and received none. Without further ado he continued with the hearing and wrote the statement on the table in chalk. When the time came for the hearings to be laid before the City Magistrate, Hafner had the table carried to him. When he was asked about it he replied that he regarded it as a matter of conscience that a person who might conceivably be innocent should not have his arrest prolonged by one day merely on account of a paper-miser.

2. ibid., p. 89.
I wasn't born for studied and regular plays, but was made (may Apollo take me!) for brilliant, extempore (comedy)."

3. ibid., p. 90ff.

4. ibid., p. 133ff.

5. ibid., p. 96.
   ". . . for the moment I can't think of a reason, and anyway I'd almost forgotten about it."
6. ibid., II, xii. p.191.
7. ibid., I, iii. p.140-141.

> CASPERL (*stops him*):
> Where are you going? Get back! Where are you going?
> BARON PAPPENDECKEL:
> I want to get into this house here.
> CASPERL:
> Are you Tom, Sir?
> BARON PAPPENDECKEL:
> I am who I am, what business is it of yours?
> CASPERL:
> It's very much my business and I've got to know whether Sir is Tom?
> BARON PAPPENDECKEL (*aside*):
> It seems to me that the fellow's been told to let no one but a certain Tom into the house, but I'll show the stupid devil. (*To Casperl.*) Well! if you really want to know, I'll tell you: yes! I am Tom.
> CASPERL (*laughs*):
> Indeed! Then Sir can be on his way, the gentleman will not be admitted.
> BARON PAPPENDECKEL:
> And why not?
> CASPERL:
> Neither Tom, Dick nor Harry is allowed in.
> BARON PAPPENDECKEL (*aside*):
> What the deuce! What a pretty mess! Now what? (*To Casperl.*) Good friend! If you let me into the house, I'll give you six ducats.
> CASPERL (*weeps*):
> Gracious Heaven, how could You let such a generous Sir be called Tom?

8. II, 3ff.
9. II, vi. (II, 55.)
10. I, iv. (II, 111.)
11. III, xv., 197.
12. I, iii., 109.
    ". . . then the period of witchcraft is over."
13. ibid., p. 33-36.

ARIA 1
Megära

Pray observe most carefully
The boundless power of my art!

Look upon it fearlessly,
For to you no harm shall come;
Though everything shall groan and split,
Be calm, and tremble not.
>   (*With her wand she makes magic circles in the air and down
>   to earth.*)
Pluto, Charon, Phlegeton,
Lethe, Stix, and Acheron,
Tantalus and Radamas,
Sisiphus and Salt-white Cheese,
Devils, Furies of Hell,
Hear my solemn command,
Be ready for my call !
>   (*A terrible cry is heard*)
Hearken to the screaming swarm !
>   (*To Hans Wurst and Leander.*)
The impossibility of things,
I often render possible;
My wand needs only to command,
And swiftly nature moveth to obey,
But once need I command,
Forthwith the water rages,
>   (*The river begins to boil.*)
In their course the waves rise up,
Waves which were so placid;
Barely is my wish made known
Than the thunder is heard to roll,
>   (*Clouds gather and cover the sun, thunder and lightning.*)
So does the lightning flash,
And the sun's heat melt away.
Trees I also bring to life;
>   (*The trees on the bank move*).
Mountains must breathe fire,
>   (*The mountain beyond the water spits out fire.*)
And a stone, given life,
Is shown to be a maiden.
>   (*The small rock near the water is transformed into a maiden.*)
The loyalty of my devils
Is beyond all disputation;
>   (*From both sides devils spring from the earth, embrace each
>   other in the middle of the stage, Death appears out of the
>   earth.*)
Behold, even cunning Death
Appears, to honour my command.
But not yet have I shown you
My strong and mighty giants.
>   (*Enter two giants.*)

Have you observed them closely?
Have they not been finely built?
Nor must any of my trolls be
Withheld from your curiosity.
Of these tormentors two
Serve ever at my table.
    (Four ugly trolls appear.)
Bears, tigers, lions, dragons,
I can change to lambs,
    (Flying dragons appear and some reptiles which settle at the
    witch's feet.)
See, how peacefully they rest!
O the dear, dear animals! *(She strokes the animals.)*
    (To Leander and Hans Wurst.)
Now you have observed,
What it is in my power to do,
Therefore spirits return,
Leave us this instant!
    (All the spirits move away, the giants go off and the trolls
    as well, the reptiles slip away, the devils embrace each other
    again and disappear. Amidst fire Death also retires, the
    dragons fly away, the dark clouds disappear, the thunder and
    lightning ceases, the sun reappears, the maiden is trans-
    formed again into a rock and the waves become calm again.)
O Nature! Return to the state
Of your previous calm!
Obey my sign
And with dispatch.
    (To Hans Wurst and Leander.)
How did you like these trivia?

14. cf., p. 16.

15. I, xi., p. 135.
You can easily learn it by heart, I need only household medicines.
Just take some scabious tea made with bugs and Rosoli cream, that
will cool you off a bit and do wonders for your constitution.
Normally it's a cordial for desperate fools and if you don't im-
prove, then in the name of Heaven, you'll simply kick the bucket.

16. II, iii. p. 44.
(To Colombine): Why do you weep my child? We are born to
die! *(Pointing at the two old men.)* Him today and him tomorrow,
Death spares no-one.
  The world has been chosen only for our torment,
  Our body's the sick-bed of our soul,
  And therefore I wish soon for the honour,
  Of burying you both by my own hand.
    (Exit solemnly.)

LEAN.: ... I know how stubborn and miserly Odoardo can be, and as I can't have Angela as my wife, she shall discover through my death how dearly I loved her and you shall keep me company in death, for I must retain a servant.

HW.: You'd be better advised to hire a part-time valet in the other world, until I follow you into it.

LEAN.: No, you've got to die with me, just think of the honour which this death will bring us. The world will place us among the heroes.

HW.: I'd much rather be numbered amongst the living cowards than the dead heroes.

LEAN.: How timorous you are, you've got to die once in any case. So get ready, or I'll shoot your soul out through your elbow.

HW. (*very afraid*): O a thousand flaming devils, it's just not done to force a fellow like this merely because you enjoy dying. It's unheard of!

LEAN.: Be silent! and listen carefully! Stay at your post, take the pistol and aim at me, then begin to count 1, 2, 3, and as soon as you say three, shoot at me, and on the dot I'll empty my barrel at you.

HW.: (*Strikes an attitude of fear and begins to count, one . . .*)

LEAN.: Stop! Before I die, I would like this little jewel to say a word or two to the Angela I worship. You could do the same honour for Colombine. My adored Angela. . .

HW.: My damned Colombine. . .

LEAN.: Because in my life I cannot possess you. . .

HW.: In my life I wish that I'd never even seen you, but since I have seen you. . .

LEAN.: So shall I out of loyalty to you, because I could not see you in the arms of another. . .

HW.: I am absolutely disgusted that now together with my mad master. I shall . . .

LEAN.: Offer up my soul.

HW.: . . . Have my soul shot at.

LEAN. (*to* HW.): Now get on with it and give the orders.

HW. (*in a ridiculous posture keeps on counting 1 and 2, but instead of arriving at 3 he begins again and again with 1, or counts 4 and 5 instead of 3.*)

LEAN.: O stop it! I see you're no more than a timid fool. I'll give the word instead.

HW. (*begins to tremble*): It's all over now.

LEAN.: Pay attention and as soon as I say three, shoot at me: 1, 2, 3. (*He fires. At the count three Hans Wurst drops the pistol before Leander has fired and falls to the ground with a great scream; at the same time the large rock on the bank at one side opens and is transformed into a magic chamber.*)

18. *Die Zauberflöte* (ZB), I, v.
"The mountains move apart and the scene changes into a magnificent room."

19. ibid., II, xxix.
. . . No-one hears me, all is still! (*Looks around.*)
So it be your will?
Papageno, string yourself up!
End your life here and now! (*Looks around.*)
No, I'll wait a bit, let's say,
Until I've counted one, two, three. (*Plays the pipes.*)
One! (*Looks round and pipes.*)
Two! (*Looks round.*)
Two's gone already! (*Plays the pipes.*)
Three! (*Looks round.*)
Well, so be it. . .

20. III, 47.

21. III, ii., p. 79.
. . . it is quite certain that Leander is gradually beginning to fall
out of favour with me, but the fault of that is not so much my
wavering heart as the many obstacles of this whole affair. . .

22. ibid., II, i., p. 38.
. . . at first sight I was yours, yet you treated me too cruelly when
by a rash deed you took away the opportunity of my possessing
you forever. With a quick flight you could have saved us both
from a tyrannical father and in so doing made us both happy. . .

23. ibid., I, vii., p. 20.
O my dear Colombine! My heart is full of dread as to how
Leander has reacted to the letter. Is he asking my father for my
hand in marriage, or has his request been refused? Cost what it
must, I shall possess Leander; without him my life is unbearable,
in him alone do I see all those qualities which can please my heart.
Behold his portrait, he is certainly not the handsomest, but he has
a certain something which must attract almost all women; do you
observe his eye, how much in love it is, and at once how solemn. o
what a beautiful eye! (*She kisses the portrait.*)

24. III, 307ff.

25. ibid., p. 306.

26. I, 1. p. 308.
PAMSTIG:
Your beseeching is in vain; stand up, or else I'll box your ears!
EVAKATHEL:
This devil's love does burn my heart,
Burns to dust and ashes; O father O—
PAMSTIG:
Be silent! Or I'll take you by your hair.

EVAKATHEL :
   Let Prince Schnudi be my man—
PAMSTIG :
   That clot?
EVAKATHEL (*stands up*) :
   Don't be so unfair !

27.   II, ix., p. 327.
SCHNUDI (*with the tartar's head.*) :
   ... But hear my innocence ! I know that I have erred,
   Your father's body from his soul severed;
   The situation forced me thus to act,
   Had I not cut him short, he would have slaughtered me ...

28.   II, ix., p. 329.
   My feelings for him now are as before too warm,
   And powerless I remain to dampen this my ardour;
   Therefore I punish in me what I cannot punish in him,
   And because I cannot get him, I'll die without a man.

29.   II, ix., p. 332.
SCHNUDI :
   My friends—Ooo twitch ! Fare-well ! Ooo I'm dying !
   O help !—Ooo twitch !—I'm bursting, I'm going !
   O Fire !—Ooo twitch !—Water quickly; Ooo twitch !
   The pain—Ooo twitch !—is increasing every moment.
   The poison—Ooo twitch !—is agony, it's tearing, it's running,
   My stomach—Ooo twitch !—is being burnt through and
      through !
   Princess !—Ooo twitch ! I'm dying—
      (*He falls to the ground and dies.*)

30.   II, 199ff.

31.   p. 220. fn.

32.   I, ix. p. 227.
   "Indeed?—Hang it all ! I can surely tell the difference between a
   dog and the wailing of a ghost—."

33.   III, vii. p. 270.
   "How happy I shall be when Valer frees me this very night from
   my mad father. . ."

34.   II, iv and v. p. 240-241.
HANS WURST (*alone, extremely irate*): Odds balls and muskets !
   Giving me a slap in the face when I'm innocent? It's not going to
   stay on my face ! I'll take it off. (*He takes a handkerchief from his
   bag, puts in on the ground, kneels down and wipes his face with
   his hands for a time, as if he is trying to get the slap into the
   handkerchief.*) Now it's off my face. (*He takes the handkerchief
   by its four corners and goes off carrying it as if he has something
   concealed inside it.*) I'll carry this slap straight home to my master; he's treated me unfairly in any case, and since I simply didn't

deserve this slap, it surely belongs to him, not to me. (*Prepares to enter his master's house.*)

Scene Five

(*Valer comes out of the house. Hans Wurst.*)

VAL. (*to* HW.): Where are you going?

HW. (*angrily*): I was coming into the house to see you.

VAL.: Did you deliver the letter? Where's the answer?

HW.: I gave the letter to Lisette and the answer is here in the handkerchief.

VAL.: You idiot! What do you mean the answer's here in the handkerchief?

HW.: It would have been too heavy for me to bear otherwise.

VAL.: Let me see! (*tears the handkerchief away from* HW., *holds it in one hand and peers into it.*) Where is it then? I can't see anything.

HW.: It"s just coming out now. (*Knocks the handkerchief into Valer's face*).

VAL. (*draws his sword*): What? You wretched dog, that'll cost you your life! . . .

35. III, x. p. 295.

Today's unexpected events and the love I bear my sister move me to postpone my departure to the regiment until the day after tomorrow.

36. II, xv., p. 256.

HW. (*seemingly deep in thought*): That's five ducats altogether, two of them belong to today, I'll return those to my master who's been tricked. (*Puts them in the bag.*) One ducat I'll tipple away for my trouble. (*Puts one away.*) One ducat expenses for a few pieces of straw and two rattan canes. (*As above.*) And one ducat goes as a tip for the two corporals who broke the barber's arm and leg. That's how it's to be shared out and the five ducats are gone. (*To the barber.*) I've rumbled your game, you indoor beast of a barber. Is that how you behave towards honest people? Is that how you choose to deceive my gracious master, who has given you so much?

FRIS. (*very afraid*): If you'll allow, Sir musketeer! You are completely wrong—it's all quite different.

HW.: What do you mean different? you damned rogue, do you think that I didn't hear all that was said between you and my master's father? But you'll see what kind of man you have to deal with. Get your whig-making soul in order for you must die. (*Draws his sabre.*)

37. cf., p. 17.

38. 1, i., p. 206.

What can there be in it of any importance other than the usual cooing-noises: my angel!—I'm pining;—my love!—my life—my

146

mistress! In my thoughts I kiss you;—my idol!—give me your heart!—I plight my eternal troth to you;—I perish; the deuce take me!—and such-like love-games. And it's all so futile. . .

39. II, 201-202.

. . . And I say without hesitation that neither Plautus nor Molière nor Holberg ever conceived a comic character more truthfully or presented him more vividly. The house-steward in Vienna is to be found in any of the larger houses; he has normally learnt the craft of masonry. In most cases he lives in the entrance-hall, he sees to the lighting on the stairs, he whitewashes the walls, sees to all the minor matters in the house, he discharges his master's obligations towards his tenants. All this leads to his being more or less familiar with the private affairs of those who live in the house, and whoever wished to enter or leave the house whilst it was locked, or had some secret business within the house, would first have to come to some arrangement with the house-steward.

40. I, ii. p. 210-211.

VAL.: I just don't know how to begin with the ass. (*To the steward.*) Listen, good friend! Is Henriette still sleeping?

HAUSM.: Aye, certainly. She will only just have gone to bed; for neither she nor I have closed our traps all night.

VAL.: Why not?

HAUSM.: What? What do you say?

VAL.: Why did you stay up all night?

HAUSM.: Indeed, quite true.

HW. (*shouts very loudly*): My worthy master would like to know how it was that you got no sleep. (*Aside.*) The fellow's got a double-door in front of his ears.

HAUSM.: I understand you now. We weren't able to sleep for the old man is so afraid of ghosts and they often come at night to talk to him; and the phantom should have appeared again last night and that's why we had to stay awake with him all night, Miss Henriette and myself; I had to watch out for the spirits, and Miss Henriette for the phantom.

VAL. (*aside*): What fools there are in the world! (*To the steward.*) But now it would be very easy for you to give Miss Henriette the letter.

HAUSM.: Yes, yes, the phantom often visits my master, climbs on to him and sucks three gills or even a whole measure of the blood she thirsts for. Afterwards she goes away again and my master is frightfully ill.

VAL.: Here is the letter, I'm asking you for the last time, will you or won't you deliver it?

HAUSM.: No, no, I cannot, I may not, I will not, I durst not, I shall not, I don't want to.

VAL. (*to the steward*): In that case just let me say this. . .

HAUSM. (*angrily*): What's that? Strike me? Strike me? It's not

147

my job to look after you. Now I'm going straight to my master to tell him—so you were going to strike me were you? (*Standing still a moment, then suddenly furious again.*) What? What? Who's a boor? I'm not a pimp—I'm an honest fellow—my master will show you what you need to be shown. (*Runs off angrily into the house.*)

41. III, p. 112ff.

42. Rommel, op. cit., p. 211ff.

43. Printed text available in the Viennese Austrian National Library. cf., also *The Work of Emanuel Schikaneder and the Tradition of the Old Viennese Popular Theatre*. E. M. Batley. (Durham University, 1965. unpubl.) III, 187ff.

44. I, i. p. 121.
. . . Nero murdered his mother with a dagger, but you, you villain, will dance your father to death. (*He weeps and immediately bursts out laughing again.*) But they struck up the waltz and I'll think of it as long as I live. . . The German dance is much more fun than the minuet. (*He begins to play a waltz on his fiddle, jumps and dances around in a lively fashion.*)

45. I, xxxviii.

46. III, 217ff.

47. III, xvi. p. 301.
Feelings of revenge, shame, regret and fear have taken a hold on my soul—on all sides I have been deceived and disgraced! What will the world—what will my acquaintances say of me? Yet what have they been able to say of me previously? What a sorry mess you're in, you poor Frau Redlich. But with all your extravagances what else could you have expected? Everything is lost!—the respect which they had for me, but who showed any, except those whom, to my own loss, I paid to show it? . .

48. *Die Briefe W. A. Mozarts und seiner Familie*, L. Schiedermair, Wiesbaden & Munich, 1914, IV, 369ff. Salzburg, November 30, 1780.

49. op. cit., p. 392.

50. ibid., p. 544ff.
cf., also *Das Theater in der Wiener Leopoldstadt 1787-1860*, F. Hadamowsky, (Kataloge der Theatersammlung der Nationalbibliothek in Wien, III, 793814—C. Th. S.) p. 57. *Memoiren meines Lebens: Gefundenes und Empfundenes, Erlebtes und Erstrebtes*, I. 1781-1813, I. F. Castelli, Vienna & Prague, 1861.

51. III, 324.

Chapter 4

THE GROWTH OF *SINGSPIEL* IN
SOUTHERN GERMANY

1. London, 1964.
2. *Geschichte der deutschen Schauspielkunst*, E. Devrient, Berlin, 1905, I, 88.
3. *Die Singspiele der englischen Komödianten und ihrer Nachfolger in Deutschland, Holland und Skandinavien*, J. Bolte, Hamburg & Leipzig, 1893, p. 51ff.
4. Komorzynski, op. cit.
5. Rommel, op. cit., p. 352ff.
6. op. cit., p. IX.
7. Rommel, op. cit., p. 363.
8. Haas, op. cit., p. 54ff.
   . . . They both met and Haydn followed Kurz into his home. "Sit down at the piano and play some suitable music to accompany the mime I'm going to do for you. Imagine that Bernardon has fallen into the water and is trying to swim to safety." Now he calls for his servant, throws himself across an arm-chair and has the servant push the chair up and down the room. He moves his arms and legs as if he is swimming whilst Haydn expresses in his music in 6/8 time the play of the waves and the swimming. Suddenly Bernardon jumps up, throws his arms round Haydn and nearly suffocates him with kisses. "Haydn, you're my man. You must write an opera for me." And thus arose *Der krumme Teufel*. Haydn was paid 25 ducats for it and thought himself very rich. The opera was performed twice and had a very warm reception but after that it was banned on account of offensive remarks in the text.
9. M. Bt. 1 p. 33ff.
10. Komorzynski, op. cit., p. 38ff.
11. Rommel, op. cit., p. 355.
12. *World of Opera*, Brockway & Weinstock (Great Britain, 1963), p. 85fn.
13. Since the public received this first attempt by an amateur of the Muses, but one who is dedicated to the stage, with some approval, so has that person been persuaded to have the play printed after making obvious improvements. Lovers of music and the theatre who have good taste, will show him by the measure of their applause whether they wish to encourage him or bid him be silent.
14. *175 Jahre Burgtheater*, Buschbeck & Judtmann (Viennese Austrian National Library) 852739-C. Th-s.
15. Komorzynski, op. cit., p. 26ff.

16. *Komische Opern*, C. F. Weisse, Leipzig, 1777.

17. *Versuch über das deutsche Singspiel und einige dahin einschlagende Gegenstände* C. M. Wieland, SW. Vol. 45, Leipzig, 1824, p. 123ff.

18. I, v.

> PROPRIETRESS :
>> Let me tell you, you ragged crew !
>> That I'm the mistress of the house.
>> Just toddle along with you !
>
> ALL :
>> Woman, we can't go like that:
>> We are guests and we pay.
>
> SCHOOLMASTER :
>> I, the schoolmaster, wish above all
>> For much more respect, much more respect,
>> For I'm a learned man.
>
> PROPRIETRESS :
>> Who's always sitting in the tavern,
>> Drinking with louts, and who knows how to tipple.
>> Be off, out of my house.
>
> SCHOOLMASTER :
>> I'm a schoolmaster.
>
> PROPRIETRESS :
>> Out of my house !
>
> PEASANT :
>> I'm a juror.
>
> PROPRIETRESS :
>> Out of my house !
>
> LEICHTSINN :
>> I'm a well-travelled—
>
> PROPRIETRESS :
>> Out of my house !
>
> STOCK :
>> I'm a born—
>
> PROPRIETRESS :
>> Out of my house !
>
> LEICHTSINN :
>> Violinist !
>
> STOCK :
>> Bass !
>
> PROPRIETRESS :
>> Out of the place ! . . .

19. II, vii.

> PROPRIETRESS : Sire ! I would willingly have let you earn something : you know, people are so strange; they see evil in every-

thing. And the schoolmaster, he always makes the most noise.
One's a better chance of allowing a good time in the evening
than in the middle of the day : I agree with it myself and I
shall be very happy to know you better.

LEICHTSINN (*kisses her hand*): You are too kind, Frau Wirthinn,
and your sky-blue eyes, blow me if they don't tempt me !

PROPRIETRESS : And your dark eyes are just as dangerous.

ARIE

One would as feelingless as stone
And not a woman be !
To see such kind dark eyes,
And under them a face
Expressing warmth and rapture;
Did one not in flames explode !

2.

If ever heart were not ravished
By this look as sweet as honey,
Whoever still would wish to be stern and melancholy :
Merits not such tender happiness.
O no ! no ! Not to be a stone
But a woman, is my desire.

20. I, i.

21. *Wort in der Zeit* 2. Jahrgang, 1956. Heft 5.

22. *Augsburger Mozartbuch* ed. H. Endrös. (Augsburg, 1942/43).

23. Komorzynski op. cit., p. 84ff.

24. ibid., p. 93ff.

25. WHTA, p. 89ff.
     Komorzynski, op. cit., p. 93ff.
     Denkmäler der Tonkunst in Österreich ed. R. Haas. No. 36. *Die Berg-
     knappen* (Vienna, 1911).

26. *Gotha Theaterkalender* 1779, p. 101-102.

27. Schiedermair, op. cit., II, 199. December 21, 1782. WM-LM.

28. Rommel, op. cit., p. 430.
     The idea represented on the curtain is quite clever. Hans Wurst is
     sitting on the left, hung with black crape, and mourns his banish-
     ment from the theatre. Towards the middle of the curtain the
     characters of the Italian theatre, Scapin, Pierrot, Harlequin and
     Dottore are dancing a round, but their arms and legs are fastened
     in chains, signifying that they are no longer so free to appear
     on the German theatre. On the right Parnassus is to be seen with
     a turn-pike, which a sullen, pedantic critic guards with a whip,
     refusing the comedians entry to Parnassus. Meanwhile Kasperl,
     accompanied by Thalia, is travelling through the air on a wingèd
     coach up Parnassus in defiance of the sullen critic; which we who
     are reasonable, who live and let live, would willingly allow.

29. *Dramatische und andere Skizzen nebst Briefen über das Theater-wesen zu Wien*, J. Schink, Vienna, 1783, IV, p. 123.
30. Hadamowsky, op. cit., p. 44ff.
31. Komorzynski, op. cit., p. 72ff.

Chapter 5

EMANUEL SCHIKANEDER AND THE VIENNESE SINGSPIEL AFTER 1789

1. Hadamowsky, op. cit., p. 51.
2. Komorzynski, op cit.
3. *Ziettafel der Erstaufführungen und anderer Ereignisse*, Vienna & Leipzig, 1937.
4. *Das deutsche Singspiel*, Leipzig & Augsburg, 1863.
5. ibid., p. 159.
   "The hitherto concise form is extended, the names Singspiel and operetta disappear, the great romantic, lyrical, comic operas take their place."
6. Deutsch, op. cit.
7. See under *Neuerbautes*:
   Substantial and prompt payment for the play immediately upon acceptance without waiting for the performance or after it, meant that the theatre never lacked plays; thus the management, as well as works by Schikaneder and several other members of its theatre, can look to expect works by better brains from home and abroad, amongst whose numbers I would quite rightly include Richter (author of the Eipeldauer letters and Austria's Rabelais) and Gewey, the author of the *Modesitten* (part two of which is to follow and whose "seltener Prozess" was so well received).
8. Komorzynski, op. cit., p. 171-172.
9. *150 Jahre Theater an der Wien*, Zürich, Leipzig & Vienna, 1952). See under *Vor-und Baugeschichte*.
10. op. cit., p. 498.
11. Marie Anne Thekla Mozart, in a letter to her brother in 1780, describes one of these rare moments of humiliation for the impresario. cf., Schiedermair, op. cit., IV, 371. MM-WM., November 30, 1780.
12. *Wiener Hoftheateralmanach 1803*, "Neuerbautes."
13. *Die Entstehung der Zauberflöte*, ed. J. Klemm., p. 444ff.
14. Copy in MSS Department, National Library, Vienna. (Series nova 58-60), December 16, 1791.

15. *Wolfgang Amadeus Mozart*, G. N. von Nissen, p. 580ff. ". . . a certain, rather famous art-dealer."

16. p. 444ff.
    ". . . Only you can save me. Mr. H., a merchant, has promised me a loan of 2,000 Fl., if you will write an opera for me. . ."

17. p. 185.

18. Deutsch, op. cit.
    Castelli, op. cit. "Das Theater auf der Wieden."

19. Komorzynski, op. cit., p. 311.

20. Deutsch, op. cit.

21. ibid.,
    Komorzynski, op. cit.
    Rommel, op. cit.

22. *Denksteine*, A. Schmidt, Vienna, 1848, p. 3ff.

23. Deutsch, op. cit.

24. ibid.

25. Komorzynski, op. cit., p. 265ff.

26. *300 Jahre Wiener Operntheater. Werk und Werden*, Pirchan/Fritz/Witischnik, Vienna, 1953, p. 37ff.
    Bauer, op. cit., "Vor-und Baugeschichte".

27. Perinet, op. cit.

28. Batley, op. cit., II, 116ff.

29.   The way is not too far,
        The river not wide at all,
        One leap and you are there!—

30. Bauer, op. cit., "Vor-und Baugeschichte".

31. *Wiener Hoftheateralmanach*, "Neuerbautes".

32. Komorzynski, op. cit., p. 326.

33. I, iii.
    Where was I? Where am I? Truly that was my worst dream yet, but also the most wonderful reawakening of a whole life-time. (*Points to the busts.*) For a long time I have born these three monuments in my heart, and forever shall they dwell unforgotten in my grateful soul. Accept my thanks, you greatest of men, most gracious of this earth! Without you, where would I be now? And you, you great ones who rule at the helm of the state—you incorruptible judges I humbly thank for your grace and kindness, for your just counsel. Thanks be to all this worthy audience for its support, for its participation in the workings of my fate. Thanks be to the friend whom as a result of his modesty I can and may not name—and who thus far has offered me a helping hand. Since I trod Thalia's rough path I have found many a good and

honest fellow, but a person who would risk such great things for the sake of a friend, must own a noble heart. So my public thanks to him. Oh, if only I—if only we might succeed in bringing pleasure and happiness to you, you esteemed patrons, that would be all that we could desire—if men can gladden us after their daily occupation —this we would wish to do—I solemnly promise it here and now— if we can offer distraction wherever possible—if we achieve this aim, then is this temple—my happiness—founded on rock.

34. Komorzynski op. cit., p. 323.

35. Pirchan op. cit., p. 37ff.
   The confusion, the trying-out and arranging for the march and the twenty-three horses, of which three were harnessed to the triumphal coach which overturned backwards and threw out the singers, Madam Campi and Herr Simoni, all of it didn't allow one even to imagine that a performance could be given on the same day.

36.   (*Open region near the city of Bezira which is to be seen in the background. In the middle of the stage a triumphal gate; the wings are an avenue of palm-trees. Hephestion marches on with Alexander's army. Out of the town, through the gateway, come the Indian people, the elders of the kingdom, ladies and townspeople, then Alexander, the Queen and the prince; before them girls and boys dance and strew flowers. Alexander's army and the Indians embrace each other*)

CHORUS

Let ring throughout the world,
Our happiness and joy!
Long live Kiasa! Long live the greatest hero!
Long lasting as today.
He gave us a golden peace,
The gods have given him to us
For our happiness and pleasure,
Our hearts beat out our thanks to you... !

37. Komorzynski does not note that the payment applied equally to Schikaneder's wife (op. cit., p. 328.). A second version of the "Vogel-fänger" aria in Act I was written by Schikaneder to celebrate the anniversary of the opening of the theatre and he sang it in the performance of *The Magic Flute* given on June 13, 1802. The following line has an obvious bearing on Schikaneder's payment: ". . . Ich weiss was zweymal fünfzig sey" (". . . I know what two times fifty are") *Wiener Hoftheateralmanach* 1803. p. 105.

38. Komorzynski, op. cit., p. 334ff.

39. See *Goethe Bicentennial Studies*, P. Nettl, Indiana, 1950.

40. "Der 'Zauberflöte' zweiter Theil", A. Bauer, Österreichische Musik-zeitschrift, Jahrgang 4, (Vienna, 1949), p. 180.

41. Komorzynski, op. cit., p. 339ff.

42. *Eipeldauerbriefe*, 5. Heft, 4. Brief, p. 48; also 6, 1, p. 7; 7, 3, p. 27; 10, 3, p. 23.

43. Komorzynski, op. cit., p. 336-337, 294-295.

44. ibid., p. 345ff.

Chapter 6

SCHIKANEDER'S VIENNESE *SINGSPIELE* PRIOR TO *THE MAGIC FLUTE*

1. J. Richter, op. cit. (Vienna, 1785, 1799, 1808.)

2. Deutsch, op. cit.

3. *Mozart—Briefe und Aufzeichnungen*, Deutsch/Bauer (Kassel, 1964), IV, 161. WM-MmeM., Vienna, June 12, 1791, p. 137.

4. I, i.

> In my slumber too I see you
> Dearest youth before me still
> Anton! hovers round about me
> And with you my soul communes,
> Named you mine, for ever mine;
> And scarce have I awakened than
> I so sadly realize,
> You were mine in dream alone.
> So do I needs hate my standing,
> Which robs you of me always,
> Which stole from me the highborn hand
> Of you my equal.

5. Gürge is in despair when Lottchen goes alone to the Prince's court and her disdainful treatment of Gürge in his lowly position is one of the rare moments of cruelty in the *Singspiel* of the strolling stage.

6. Barthel, a village barber, is already married before the action of the play begins. He and his wife have their arguments but their genuine love for each other is seen as the happy solution for all things.

7. O night! blacker by far than hell
> Death and despair rage here,
> No ray of light streams through the hell
> Of pent-up grief within me.
>
> I am the victim of my love.
> I'm racked by untellable pain,
> O if only you could feel my desires,
> For 'tis in vain that my heart feels them.
>
> There's no advice and I am lost,
> My reasoning too beyond repair,
> Ever to grieve was I born,
> Welcome death! Give me your hand.

155

Trembling, down to the stream,
Let not my brains spurt in the water;
So does your suffering end.

Away Anton! away! never falter,
What use my fearful hesitation,
What use be my lamenting,
Josepha! Father! fare you well!

8. How often do women trap men in their snare,
    Lying and cheating they do everywhere,
    Apoplexy they give me and also gall-fever,
    O women! O women! O women!...

9. "A woman's the finest creation on earth..."

10. A woman's the finest creation on earth,
    Who denies it, I'll beat him and push his face in...
        (As the courier rides in with the news of the Prince of Ko-
        burg's victory.)
    One hears almost daily something new in the world,
    Above all of our young soldiers in action.
    I've just seen, as I went into the city
    Many riders wearing their fine red coats,
    They went treng, teng, teng, as they spurred them along,
    And one there I asked what was going on?
    He replied that Koburg, our mighty hero
    Had beaten the Turk and pushed his face in...

11. All the good old times are gone
    When I was fancy free
    And when I worked but for myself.
    Now the little shower cries at me,
    And then the wife will fill my ear,
    The deuce, the noise I cannot bear...

12. Komorzynski op. cit., p. 3-4.

13. What happiness never felt before
    I'm crowned today with love and wealth
    With money and with property I'm by
    This fairest maiden in the world enriched.
    Love and gold, and gold and love
    Are the highest endeavours of men.
    Truly I'm beside myself
    For I'm smiled on by gold and love.

14. Sofrano, my son! Your father is talking to you; your womanly
    behaviour has been weighed and as a result all help refused you.
    Yet if you wish to succeed, well then, be a man and with all the
    power you can muster, pursue the enemy; if by your arm he is
    robbed of his power, then I personally will wind the garland
    around your head. (He disappears amidst thunder and lightning,
    the pillar stands as it was previously.)

156

15. *Dschinnistan,* ed. C. M. Wieland (Winterthur, 1786, 1787, 1789).

16. Schiedermair, op. cit., IV, 159; LM-WM, December 11, 1780.

> I recommend you in your work not to think only of the musicians in the audience, but also of those *who are not musicians,* you should know that there are always 100 *ignoramuses* as against 10 *true connoisseurs.* Therefore don't forget the so-called *popular* style which will tickle also the *long ears.*

17. ibid., II, 125; WM-LM, December 16, 1780.

> . . . don't worry about the so-called popular style, for in my opera there's music for all kinds of people—except for those with long ears.

18. Castelli op. cit.

> It's laughable what Schikaneder is supposed to have answered to a friend who had praised his work after the première of *The Magic Flute.* He is supposed to have said: "Yes, the opera was well received, but it would have had an even better reception if Mozart hadn't ruined so much of it for me. . ."

19. *Kleine Wiener Memoiren,* 3. Theil, F. Gräffner (Vienna, 1845), p. 21.

20. *Aus Mozarts Freundes- und Familienkreis,* E. K. Blümml (Vienna, 1923), p. 119.

21. Komorzynski, op. cit.
    Rommel, op. cit., p. 152.

22. op. cit., p. 21.

> He was dissatisfied with many things, a keen critic with a practical head on his shoulders, who knew his audience. A hundred times this practical head made its incisions into Mozart's genius. Not so learned, my friend, that's too lofty for people; you must make it simpler, more natural, and the genius did as his Brother and director demanded. The duet: "Bey Männern, welche Liebe fühlen. . ." Mozart had to alter, completely recast and reshape no less than four times, and even then it wasn't right for the man of strict rhythm. That's all too learned, he decided; I want it like this, and sang him the duet as he wanted it and needed it, and—as Mozart in fact adopted and composed it, just as we have it now. "The duet," declared Schikaneder, "is by me." (No less are most of the Papageno songs by him.)

23. Rommel, op. cit.
    Komorzynski, op. cit.
    Blümml, op. cit., "Gratulatorisches Quodlibet".

24. Castelli, op. cit., "Das Theater auf der Wieden".

> Schikaneder was a wretched singer, and for this reason he either wrote the melody to those parts which he had to sing himself in his opera, or he told the composer what to write. Thus the melodies in *The Magic Flute* to the songs "Der Vogelfänger bin ich ja" and "Ein Mädchen oder Weibchen", and also the duet "Bei Män-

nern welche Liebe fühlen" are by Schikaneder. Mozart it was, however, who made them works of art by his marvellous setting.

25. Nissen, op. cit., p. 551.

26. Komorzynski, op. cit., p. 224.

27. *Mozart in Retrospect*, A. Hyatt-King (Oxford, 1955), p. 141-163. "The Melodie Sources and Affinities of *Die Zauberflöte.*"

28. Perinet, op. cit., p. 5-7.

Mozart

I know, my music betrayed me,
Both of us knew what we were doing:
You sang me many a melody first—
Admittedly it was I who afterwards produced it;
But you chose me at that time
When many a charlatan cheated me,
You understood what I was capable of.
You were a friend of the truest mould.
You gave me the opportunity to show my worth
And I made your plan my own.
Just laugh at them when they now criticize and curse,
I was there why did they not seek me?
You sought me and I found you,
Allied together we produced a great work:
There they stood around with eyes and nostrils wide,
And now they wish to blow their poison at you.
HERE you were the first, none before you,
You were the father, I the tutor;
Had the father produced no child,
It would have been good-night to its upbringing...

29. Rommel, op. cit., p. 513, fn. 49.

You Mozart! That's no good, the music must express more astonishment, first of all they've both to stare at each other in silence, then Papageno must begin to stutter: Pa-pa pa pa-pa; Papageno has got to repeat this until finally they both pronounce the whole name.

30. Schiedermair, op. cit., II, 351.

I have just come from the opera; it was just as full as ever. The duet "Mann und Weib" etc. . . . and the Glockenspiel in the first act were repeated as usual—as was the genii's trio in act two— but what gives me most satisfaction is the silent applause! One can see how much this opera is improving more and more.

Chapter 7

THE MAGIC FLUTE AND ITS DISPUTED AUTHORSHIP

1. Ch. "Die Zauberflöte-Solved", p. 131.
2. *Wolfgang Amadeus Mozart*, 4 vols., (Leipzig, 1856.)
3. p. 548f. Cf., pp. 80, 81.
4. op. cit., p. 979ff.
5. ibid., p. 979ff.
6. Komorzynski, op. cit., p. 180.
7. Rommel, op. cit., p. 985. Both versions of the libretto are available in the theatre archives of the Austrian National Library in Vienna.
8. Komorzynski, op. cit., p. 170-181.
9. p. 292ff.
10. Komorzynski, op. cit., p. 281-287.
11. ibid., p. 302ff. *Der "Zauberflöte" zweiter Theil* ed. A. Bauer, "Österreichische Musikzeitschrift", Jg. 4. (Vienna, 1949) p. 181.
12. Wieland, op. cit., II.
13. Komorzynski, op. cit., p. 333.
14. ibid., p. 61. Komorzynski sees Lessing's *Minna von Barnhelm* as having a decided influence on Schikaneder's comedy *Das Regenspurger Schif.*
15. ibid., p. 138. Schiller's *Fiesco* is also mentioned by the same authority as an influence on Schikaneder's *Der Bucentaurus oder die Vermählung mit dem Meere.*
16. *Der Text zu Mozart's "Zauberflöte" und Johann Georg Karl Giesecke*, F. Grandaur, Separat-Abdruck aus den Bayrischen Literaturblättern. Viennese City Library, 31497A. p. 7.
17. Hamburg, 1849.
18. ibid., p. 22ff.
   And above all the truly German *Magic Flute* by Schikaneder and Giesecke, a member of the chorus who did the plan of the plot, the division of scenes and the well-known simple rhymes for him.
19. Rommel, op. cit., p. 981-983. "Ist Cornets Bericht glaubwürdig?"
20. Castelli, op. cit.
   "Herr Giesecke had no real special function but played just what he had to..."
21. Cornet, op. cit., p. 22ff.
   On this occasion we discovered a lot about the old times; amongst other things we learnt to see in him (who at that time had belonged to the prohibited order of freemasons) the real author of *The Magic Flute*, (which moreover Seyfried already suspected.) I'm

relating all this according to his own statement which we had no reason to doubt. He told us all about this when I sang the cavatina inserted in *Der Spiegel von Arkadien*. Many thought that the prompter Helmböck had collaborated with Schikaneder. But Giesecke corrected us on this point too, only the figure of Papageno and his counterpart did he attribute to Schikaneder.

22. op. cit., p. 981-983.

23. A Schmidt op. cit., p. 5ff.

24. Rommel op. cit., p. 981.

Indeed Schikaneder had had no literary education but had at his disposal a natural talent and an uncommonly fertile imagination.

25. *Wiener Theateralmanach*, 1803, "Neuerbautes"

And here a rumour is to be discounted which has been falsely and widely circulated, namely that Schikaneder was not the father and fabricator of his own theatrical children. It has been proved that the plot and the dialogue are his own and Herr Winter, who at the same time is the stage-manager of the theatre, will affirm this, for he and he alone perhaps can read Schikaneder's hieroglyphs which he is the first to receive for copying.

26. I, iii.

SCHIKANEDER : Accept my thanks, you greatest of men, most gracious of this earth ! Without you, where would I be now?— and you, you great ones who rule at the helm of the state, you incorruptible judges I humbly thank you for your grace and kindness, for your just counsel. . .

27. op. cit., IV, 603. fn. 20.

Chapter 8

THE UNITY OF SCHIKANEDER'S LIBRETTO

1. *The Opera Guide*, A. Jacobs & S. Sadie, London, 1964, p. 44-45. Brophy, op. cit., p. 144f.

2. *Mozart's Opera, The Magic Flute*, E. J. Dent, Cambridge, 1911. *Mozart's Opera, a Critical Study*, E. J. Dent, London, 1913.

3. op. cit., IV, 563, 591. Treitschke. Orpheus mus. Taschenb. 1841. p. 242ff.

4. Cornet, op. cit.

5. op. cit., IV, 563. "Illustr. Familienbuch des österr. Lloyd" 1852, II, p. 119f.

6. *Monatschrift für Theater und Musik*, September, 1857.

7. p. 44ff.

8. op. cit., p. 21.

9. Castelli, op. cit.
   Rommel, op. cit., p. 981.

10. p. 553.
   "It is impossible for Mozart to have created even the slightest part of his music before the character, situation and words were in front of him."

11. Jahn, op. cit., IV, 595ff.

12. Grandaur, op. cit., p. 7.

13. Deutsch & Bauer, op. cit., IV., p. 137.
   ". . . —to cheer myself up I went to see the new opera *The Bassoonist*, which is causing such a stir—but there's nothing to it."

14. *Die Zauberflöte*, ed. Kurt Soldan, Frankfurt, London, New York, 1932, p. 59-60.
   Tis not for us to tell you this;
   Be resolute, forbearing and reticent.
   Think on this; in short, be a man,
   Then, youth, you will conquer like a man.

15. ibid., p. 61.

16. ibid., p. 61-62.
   I venture bravely through the gate,
   My intentions are noble, pure and good.
   Tremble cowardly villain !
   'Tis my duty to rescue Pamina.

17. ibid., p. 63.
   These words ring with high purport !
   But how will you find these things?
   Love and virtue are not your promptings,
   For death and revenge inflame you.

18. ibid., p. 64.
   Explain yourself further to me,
   Some delusion has deceived you.

19. ibid., p. 65-66.
   PRIEST :
      . . . Sarastro you hate?
   TAMINO :
      I shall indeed hate him ever.
   PRIEST :
      Give me your reasons.
   TAMINO :
      He is a monster, a tyrant.
   PRIEST :
      Has what you say been proved?
   TAMINO :
      Shown by a wretched woman,
      Whom grief and sorrow oppress.

PRIEST :
So a woman has turned your head?
Women do little, but talk a lot.
O youth do you believe their play of tongues?
If only Sarastro could tell you
The reason for his action.

20. ibid., p. 67.
O eternal night, when will you disperse?
When will the light find my eye?

21. _The Sudden Transformation_
Why was revenge so quickly changed into friendship?
Because—so says the prompter, three pages were left out.

22. Schiedermair, op. cit., II, 265. WM-Prof. Anton Klein, March 21,
1785. Komorzynski, op. cit.

23. op. cit., "Vorbericht".

24. (Reclam) p. 12.

25. Cornet, op. cit., p. 20ff.

26. p. 551.
. . . The high pitch of the Queen of Night's part is a touchstone
for high falsetto voices; for melodic singing and gentle sustaining
of notes, Mozart in his wisdom decided, were not appropriate for
for this revengeful Queen.

27. Komorzynski op. cit., p. 158.
"a lazy, coarse person who looks as if butter wouldn't melt in her
mouth".

28. Blümml, op. cit., p. 128.

29. Batley, op. cit., III, 171ff.

30. _Die Zauberflöte_, 1794, C. V. Vulpius, Austrian National Library
628920-A. Th. S.
Die Zauberflöte in der Weimarer Fassung der Goethe-Zeit, 1794,
628921 B. Th. S.

31. p. 177.
The rays of the sun dispel the night,
Destroy the usurped power of the deceiver.

32. p. 110.
I know all too well—I know that your soul is as black as your face.
I would moreover punish you most severely for this evil undertaking, had not an evil woman, who nevertheless has a good
daughter, forged the dagger for you. Just thank the evil meddling
of woman that you leave this place unpunished. Go!

33. Brophy, op. cit., p. 144ff.

34. Rommel, op. cit., p. 908.

35. Vulpius, op. cit., "Vorrede".

36. ibid., p. 15.
    Well then! You must surely know that Sarastro's brother was the Queen of Night's husband? that he died and left behind no son only a daughter? that the kingdom demands a *male* regent? that a woman cannot rule here, and that therefore Sarastro followed his brother in government? and that the Queen of Night, apart from her jointure and inheritance of the kingdom and of the night (*aside*) O! Simpleton that I am. (*Plays his pipes.*)

37 ibid., p. 1 "Vorrede".
    "The original play has no plan at all. The people in it go off merely to come on again, and come on merely to go off again. . ."

38. I, ii, iii.

39. op. cit., p. 16.
    PAPAGENO: Believe me! the only reason for the veil is to lead an honest fellow up the garden path.
    THE THREE LADIES (*menacingly*): Papageno!
    PAPAGENO: They don't like that. Women never like to hear the truth if it concerns their charms. (*To the Ladies.*)

40. pp. 552-553.
    Can the purest language of Sarastro's singing and the priests' choruses ever flow more deeply, with all the passion of remote wisdom? One cannot be deceived: only the calm world of initiates can sing such notes. On the other count one hears the Queen of Night, portrayed half-way already in the singing of her three veiled Ladies; nobly and proudly does her song begin, enticing the youth whom she is seeking to win and whom she ensnares with the tinsel of female vanity. Glowing with revenge, agitated by all dark passions, commanding as mother and queen, the ruler of night appears in the second aria. Only a Queen flaming with stars can sing such an aria.

41. p. 944ff.
    . . . where they (the three Ladies) point out to him (Tamino) the three young boys who will guide him, and hence are in the service of the Queen, whilst in the further course of the opera they become the creatures of Sarastro and protect Tamino and Pamina from the dark intrigues of the Queen. . .

42. By Wieland's close friend "Herr von E**" p. 35ff.

BIBLIOGRAPHY
(chronologically arranged)

Ollapatrida des durchgetrieben Fuchsmundi, J. A. Stranitzky, Vienna, 1711.

Lustige Reyss-Beschreibung/aus Saltzburg in veirschiedene Länder, J. A. Stranitzky, Vienna, 1717.

Lisuart und Dariolette, D. Schiebeler, Kraus, Vienna, 1766.

Briefe über die Wienerische Schaubühne, J. Sonnenfels, bey J. Kurtzböck, Vienna, 1768.

Theaterkalender, publ. C. W. Ettinger, Gotha, 1776.

Die Lyranten, E. Schikaneder. bey Johann T. E. von Trattner, Innsbruck, 1776.

Der Bettelstudent, P. Weidmann, J. T. E. von Trattner, Vienna, 1776.

Theaterkalender, publ. C. W. Ettinger, Gotha, 1777.

Komische Opern, C. F. Weisse and J. A. Hiller. Im Verlage der Dykischen Buchhandlung, Leipzig, 1777.

Theaterkalender, publ. C. W. Ettinger, Gotha, 1778.

Die Bergknappen, P. Weidmann, bey dem Logenmeister, Vienna, 1778.

Theaterkalender, publ. C. W. Ettinger, Gotha, 1779.

Lottchen am Hofe, C. F. Weisse and J. A. Hiller, Leipzig, 1777.

Der Dorfbarbier, C. F. Weisse and J. A. Hiller, Leipzig, 1777.

Das Regensburger Schiff, E. Schikaneder. o. Verl, Salzburg, 1780.

Die Raubvögel, E. Schikaneder, publ. J. J. Mayres, Salzburg, 1782.

Das Laster kömmt an Tage, E. Schikaneder. publ. J. J. Mayres, Salzburg, 1783.

Dramatische und andere Skizzen nebst Briefen über das Theaterwesen zu Wien, ed. J. Schink. Sonnleithnerische Buchhandlung, Vienna, 1783.

Helena und Paris, "Verfasser C. F. R." (?) adapted by E. Schikaneder. mus. P. Winter. o. Verl, Pressburg, 1784.

Die Briefe eines Eipeldauers an seinen Herrn Vetter in Kakran über d' Wienerstadt, J. Richter. bey P. Rehms, Vienna, 1785.

Die Luftbälle, oder die Liebhaber à la Montgolfier, C. F. Bretzner, Munich, 1786.

Die Luftschiffer, M. Blumhofer. bey C. H. Stage, Augsburg, 1786.

Der Grandprofos, E. Schikaneder. In der Montagischen Buchhandlung, Regensburg, 1787.

Hanns Dollinger, E. Schikander. In der Montagischen Buchhandlung, Regensburg, 1787.

Dschinnistan, 3 vols. ed. C. M. Wieland, H. Steiner & Co., Winterthur, 1786, 1787, 1789.

Arien aus dem dummen Gärtner, E. Schikaneder. Ludwig, Vienna, 1790.

Die Zauberflöte (ms.), Viennese Austrian National Library. M. 807. Th. S. No. 1379 (276, 659) (1791).

Der Fagottist, J. Perinet and W. Müller. Gedruckt bey M. A. Schmidt, Vienna, 1791.

Arien und Duetten aus dem wohltätigen Derwisch, E. Schikaneder, publ. M. Ludwig, Vienna, 1791.

Der heimliche Botschafter, (series nova 58-60), December 16, Vienna, 1791.

Die getreuen Unterthanen, E. Schikander. bei A. Doll, Vienna and Leipzig, 1792.

Herzog Ludwig von Steyermark, E. Schikaneder. A. Doll, Vienna and Leipzig, 1792.

Oberon oder König der Elfen, S. Seyler. Deutsche Schaubühne, 4. Jhg. Bd. 11. Augsburg, 1792.

Der redliche Landmann, E. Schikaneder. Steinsberg, Vienna, 1792.

Die Zauberflöte, C. V. Vulpius. bey J. S. Heinsius, Leipzig, 1794.

Weiner Theateralmanach, ed. J. Sonnleithner. Kurzbeck, Vienna, 1796.

Der unruhige Wanderer, K. F. Hensler. Gedruckt mit Schmidtischen Schriften. Vienna, 1796.

Der Tyroler Wastel, E. Schikaneder. publ. A. Geers, Leipzig, 1798.

Der wiederaufgelebte Eipeldauer, J. Richter. bey P. Rehm, Vienna, 1799.

Mozart und Schikaneder. Ein theatralisches Gespräch über die Aufführung der Zauberflöte im Stadttheater, J. Perinet. Gedruckt mit Albertischen Schriften, Vienna, 1801.

Alexander, E. Schikaneder. Gedruckt mit Albertischen Schriften, Vienna, 1801.

Thespis, E. Schikaneder. o. Verl, Vienna, 1801.

Thespis Traum, E. Schikaneder. o. Verl, Vienna, 1801.

Ein theatralisches Gespräch zwischen Mozart und Schikaneder über den Verkauf des Theaters, J. Perinet. publ. J. Riedl, Vienna, 1802.

Wiener Theateralmanach, ed. J. Perinet. bey J. Riedl, Vienna, 1803.

Wiener Hoftheateralmanach, ed. P. J. Schalbacher, Vienna, 1804.

Wiener Theaterzeitung, hg. Christiani and Bolthart, Trieste, Vienna, 1806.

Oberon. König der Elfen, K. L. Giesecke. publ. J. B. Wallishauser, Vienna, 1806.

Wiener Theateralmanach, ed. J. A. Gleich. bey J. Riedl, Vienna, 1807.

Schembera, Herr von Boskowitz, E. Schikaneder. publ. J. G. Trassler, Brünn, 1808.

Briefe des jungen Eipeldauers an seinen Herrn Vetter in Kakran, J. Richter. bey. P. Rehm, Vienna, 1808.

Philipp Hafners Gesammelte Schriften, ed. J. Sonnleithner, J. B. Wallishausser, Vienna, 1812.

Der Spiegel von Arkadien, E. Schikaneder. Gedruckt mit Zängl'schen Schriften, Munich, 1814.

Wiener Theateralmanach, ed. J. A. Gleich. bey J. Riedl, Vienna, 1814.

Oberon, C. M. Wieland. In der Weidmannischen Buchhandlung, Leipzig, 1819.

Biographie W. A. Mozarts, G. N. v. Nissen. hg. Constanze, Wittwe von Nissen. Breitkopf and Härtel, Leipzig, 1828.

Kleine Wiener Memoiren. 3. Theil, F. Gräffner. Becks Universitäts-Buchhandlung, Vienna, 1845.

Denksteine, Dr. A. Schmidt. Verlegt von der Mechitaristen-Congregation, Vienna, 1848.

Die Oper in Deutschland, J. Cornet. Meissner and Schirges, Hamburg, 1849.

The Magic Flute, tr. J. W. Mould. ed. W. S. Rocksto. T. Boosey & Co., London, 1852.

W. A. Mozart, 4 vols. O. Jahn. Breitkopf and Härtel, Leipzig, 1856.

Monatschrift für Theater und Musik, Jhrg. 3. ed. J. Klemm. B. Wallishausser, Vienna, 1857.

Don Juan, komisch-tragische Oper in zwei Akten, tr. Dr. W. Viol. Verlag von F. E. C. Leuckart, Breslau, 1858.

Memoiren meines Lebens: Gefundenes und Enpfundenes, Erlebtes und Erstrebtes, I. F. Castelli. Kober and Markgraf, Vienna and Prague, 1861.

Das deutsche Singspiel, H. M. Schletterer. Breitkopf and Härtel, Leipzig and Augsburg, 1863.

Biographisches Lexikon des Kaiserthums Oesterreich, 29. Theil C. v. Wurzbach. k.k. Hof-und Staatsdruckerei, Vienna, 1875.

Vom Wiener Volkstheater, F. Schlögl. publ. K. Proschaska, Vienna, 1883.

Die Singspiele der englischen Komödianten und ihrer Nachfolger in Deutschland, Holland und Skandinavien, J. Bolte. publ. L. Voss, Hamburg and Leipzig, 1893.

Deutsch-österreichische Literaturgeschichte, Nagl and Zeidler, Verlag Fromme. Vienna, 1899.

Geschichte der deutschen Schauspielkunst, E. Devrient. Elsner, Berlin, 1905.

Die Zauberflöte in der Weimarer Fassung der Goethe-Zeit, ed. H. Loewenfeld, Gesellschaft der Bibliophilen, Leipzig, 1908.

Denkmäler der Tonkunst in Osterreich, ed. R. Haas, No. 36, Vienna, 1911.

Mozart's Opera, The Magic Flute, E. Dent, Cambridge, 1911.

Die Zauberflöte, ed. H. Abert. Ernst Eulenburg, Leipzig, 1912.

Mozart's Operas, A Critical Study, E. Dent. Chatto and Windus, London, 1913.

Wolfgang Amadeus Mozart. Sein Leben und sein Werk, A. Schurig, Insel Verlag, Leipzig, 1913.

Memoiren meines Lebens. Gefundenes und Empfundenes. Erlebtes und Erstrebtes. I. F. Castelli. Neuauflage G. Müller, Munich, 1913.

Die Briefe W. A. Mozarts und seiner Familie, ed. L. Schiedermair. bey G. Müller, Wiesbaden and Munich, 1914.

Diplomatic Study. Frederick the Great and Kaiser Joseph, H. W. V. Temperley. Duckworth, 1915.

Die dramatische Idee in Mozarts Operntexten, H. Cohen. bei B. Cassirer, Berlin, 1915.

Der Tyroler Wastel, Alt-Wiener Volkstheater I. O. Rommel. Sonderausgabe der Deutsch-Österreichischen Klassiker-Bibliothek, Teschen, Leipzig, Vienna, 1917.

Die Zauberflöte, M. Pirker. Wiener Literarische Anstalt, Vienna, Berlin, 1920.

Altwiener Theaterlieder, ed. R. Smekal. Wiener Literarische Anstalt, Vienna and Berlin, 1920.

Das deutsche Vaudeville, F. Liebstoeckl. Selbstverl. Phil. Diss., Vienna, 1923.

Aus Mozarts Freundes- und Familienkreis, E. K. Blümml, Ed. Strache Verlag, 1923.

Die Musik in der Wiener deutschen Stegreifkomödie, R. Haas. Universal-Edition. A. G., Vienna, 1925.

Alt-Wiener Thespiskarren, Gugitz and Blümml. Anton Schroll & Co. Vienna, 1925.

Das Schauspiel der Wanderbühne, W. Flemming. Deutsche Literatur: Reihe Barock; Barockdrama. Bd. 3, Leipzig, 1931.

Barocktradition auf dem österreichisch-bayrischen Volkstheater, O. Rommel. Sammlung deutscher Literatur, Reclam. 6 vols., Vienna, 1931f.

Die Zauberflöte, ed. K. Soldan. C. F. Peters, Frankfurt, London and New York, 1932.

Mozart und die Wiener Logen, O. Deutsch. Herausgegeben von der Grossloge von Wien, Vienna, 1932.

The Revolutionary Emperor, S. K. Padover. Jonathan Cape, London, 1934.

Die Zauberflöte. Unbekannte Handschriften und seltene Drucke aus der Frühzeit von Mozarts Oper, ed. F. Brukner. Gilhofer and Ranschburg, Vienna, 1934.

Mozart, E. Blom. J. M. Dent & Sons Ltd., London, 1935.

Germany in the Eighteenth Century, W. H. Bruford, Cambridge, 1935.

Comedy in Germany in the First Half of the Eighteenth Century, B. Aitkin-Sneath, Oxford, 1936.

Das Freihaustheater auf der Wieden (1787-1801), O. E. Deutsch. Gottlieb Gistel & Co., Vienna and Leipzig, 1937.

Letters of Mozart and his Family, ed. E. Anderson, Macmillan & Co., London, 1938.

Literaturgeschichte des deutschen Volkes, J. Nadler, Berlin, 1939.

Wiener Volkskunde, L. Schmidt. Gerlach & Weidling, Vienna and Leipzig, 1940.

Augsburger Mozartbuch, 55. und 56. Bd. ed. H. Endrös. J. A. Schlossersche Buchhandlung, Augsburg, 1942-1943.

Mozart, his character, his work, A. Einstein. Oxford University Press, New York, 1945.

Mozart, B. Paumgartner. Atlantis Verlag, Freiburg and Zürich, 1945.

Der "Zauberflöte" zweiter Theil, E. Schikaneder. mus. P. Winter. ed. A. Bauer. Österreichische Musikzeitschrift. Jhrg. 4, Vienna, 1949.

Goethe Bicentennial Studies, ed. H. J. Meesen. University of Indiana, Indiana, 1950.

Emanuel Schikaneder, E. Komorzynski. L. Doblinger, Wiesbaden and Vienna, 1951.

Die Alt-Wiener Volkskomödie, O. Rommel. Anton Schroll, Vienna, 1952.

Der rätselhafte Giesecke, O. E. Deutsch. Die Musikforschung, hg. im Auftrag der Gesellschaft für Musikforschung. Bärenreiter Verlag, Kassel and Basel, July, 1952.

150 Jahre Theater an der Wien, A. Bauer, Amalthea Verlag, Zürich, Leipzig and Vienna, 1952.

300 Jahre Wiener Operntheater, Pirchan/Witischnik/Fritz, Fortuna Verlag, Vienna, 1953.

Kobbé's Complete Opera Book, ed. and rev. by Earl of Harewood, Putnam, 1954.

175 Jahre Burgetheater (1776-1951), hg. mit. Unterstützung der Bundestheaterverwaltung. Viennese Austrian National Library 852739-C. Th. S., Vienna, 1954.

Wolfgang Amadeus Mozart. Eine Biographie, E. Schenk. Amalthea Verlag, Zürich, Leipzig and Vienna, 1955.

Über das Licht in der Zauberflöte, O. Kokoschka. Aus "Kokoschka. Entwürfe für die Gesamtausstattung zu W. A. Mozarts Zauberflöte". Galerie Welz, Salzburg, 1955.

Mozart in Retrospect, A. Hyatt King. Oxford University Press, 1955.

W. A. Mozart, P. Nettl. Fischer Bücherei, Hamburg, 1955.

Wort in der Zeit, Heft. 5. Jhrg. 2, Vienna, 1956.

W. A. Mozart, Neue Ausgabe sämtlicher Werke, Serie 11. Bühnenwerke. Werkgruppe 6. Bd. 1. Chöre und Zwischenaktmusiken zu Thamos, König in Ägypten. ed. F. H. Neumann Bärenreiter Verlag, Kassel and Basel, 1957.

Oxford Companion to the Theatre, ed. P. Hartnoll. Oxford University Press, 1957.

W. A. Mozart, Neue Ausgabe sämtlicher Werke, Serie 11. Bühnenwerke. Werkgruppe 5. Bd. 10. Zaïde. (Das Serail) ed. F. H. Neumann. Bärenreiter Verlag, Kassel, Basel and London, 1957.

Das Theater in der Josefstadt, A. Bauer. Manutiuspresse, Vienna and Munich, 1957.

Die Zauberflöte, ed. W. Zentner. Reclam Verlag, Stuttgart, 1957.

From Joseph II to the Jacobin Trials, E. Wangermann. Oxford University Press, 1959.

Mozart. Die Dokumente seines Lebens, ed. O. E. Deutsch. Bärenreiter Verlag, Basel, London and New York, 1961.

Composers of Operetta, G. Hughes. Macmillan & Co., London, 1962.

World of Opera, Brockway & Weinstock. Methuen & Co., Great Britain, 1963.

Mozart the Dramatist, B. Brophy. Faber & Faber, London, 1964.

The Opera Guide, A. Jacobs and S. Sadie, London, 1964.

The author was not able to establish dates of publication for the following:

Idomeneus König von Creta, W. A. Mozart. Bei. G. M. Meyer jr. (Brunswick). Zweite Aufl. bei L. I. Ewer & Co., London, 18 . . . ?

Der Text zu Mozarts "Zauberflöte" und Johann Georg Karl Giesecke, F. Grandaur. Seperat-Abdruck aus den Bayerischen Literaturblättern, Vienna City Library.

Das Theater in der Leopoldstadt (1787-1860), F. Hadamowsky. (aus: Kataloge der Theatersammlung der Nationalbibl. in Wien, Bd. III) 793814-C. Th. S.

INDEX

Afflisio, Guiseppe d', 26, 32, 33
Anfossi, Pasquale, 73
    Il curioso indiscreto, 73
Anseaume, Louis, 66
    La Clochette, 66
Ayrenhoff, Kornelius Hermann
    von, 31
    Hermann und Thusnelde, 31
    Der Postzug, 31
    Aurelius, 31

Banks, 75
    Die Gunst der Fürsten, 75
Bauernfeld, Josef von, 79, 121
Beethoven, Ludwig van, 81, 84,
    88, 91, 104
    Piano Concerto in C Major op.
    15, 84
    Christus am Ölberg, 91
    Fidelio, 91, 104
    Violin Concerto in D Minor op.
    61, 91
Bellini, 62
Bender, Freiherr von, 32
Bernardon, 20-25, 28-30, 63
Blumhofer, Max, 72
    Die Luftschiffer oder der Straf-
    planet der Erde, 72
Böhm, Johannes, 34, 72
Borosini, Francesco, 19, 62, 64
Brandes, Johann Christian, 78
    Ariadne auf Naxos, 78
Braun, Peter Freiherr von, 85-87,
    111, 112
Brenner, Anton, 21, 30, 47, 56-59
Bretzner, Christoph Friedrich, 83
    Belmont und Constanze, 83
Brezner, 72
    Die Luft bälle oder die Lieb-
    haber à la Montgolfier, 72
Burgtheater, 29, 30, 35, 36

Cervantes, Saavedra Miguel de, 67
    Die Höhle von Cuenço, 67
Chaucer, Geoffrey, 65, 66

    Tale of the Wife of Bath, 65, 66
Claudius, Matthias, 108
Coffey, Charles, 65, 66
    The Devil to Pay, 65, 66
Colombina, 21, 22, 28, 29, 33, 44,
    48
Collé, Charles, 66
    La partie de chasse de Henri IV,
    66
Commedia dell 'arte, 14, 15, 19, 20,
    21, 38, 49, 54, 56, 58, 62, 64
Corneille, Pierre, 31
    Polyeucte, 31
Corneille, Thomas, 28, 29
    Graf Essex, 28, 29

Da Ponte, Lorenzo, 83
    Figaro, 73, 94
    Così fan tutte, 83
    Don Giovanni, 83
Dryden, John, 65
Durazzo, Jacob Graf, 30, 37

Englische Comödianten, 13, 14, 61,
    62
Ewald, Johannes, 72
    Balders Tod, 72

Favart, Charles Simon, 66
    Le caprice amoureux ou Ninette
    à la cour, 66
    Annette à Lubin, 66
Freihaustheater (Theater auf der
    Wieden), 43, 60, 61, 76, 77-
    87, 93, 99, 106, 110, 111

Gay, John, 65
    The Beggar's Opera, 65
Gerl, Thaddäus, 84, 97
    Der Stein der Weisen oder die
    Zauberinsel, 84, 107
    Die verdeckten Sachen, 95f
    Der wohltätige Derwisch, 97-99,
    107
Giesecke, Johann Georg Karl, 79,
    83, 105-113, 116

171

Oberon, König der Elfen, 83, 116
Gluck, Christoph Willibald, 62, 75, 84
Die Pilgrime von Mekka, 75
Goethe, Johann Wolfgang von, 19, 90
Götz von Berlichingen, 19
Goldoni, Carlo 28
Gottsched, Johann Gottsched, 27
Versuch einer kritischen Dichtkunst, 27

Hafner, Philipp, 20, 22, 30, 37-60, 64, 67, 74, 77, 82, 94, 97, 98, 117, 122, 127
Etwas zum Lachen im Fasching, 22, 47, 56-58, 59, 77
Die Bürgerliche Dame, 30, 58-59, 77, 94
Der alte Odoardo, 38, 39
Der geplagte Odoardo, 38, 39, 74, 77, 117
Megära die förchterliche Hexe, 39-46, 97, 108
Evakathel und Schnudi, 47, 49-51
Der Furchtsame, 51-56, 58, 77, 98
Der beschäftigte Hausregent, 77
Haibel, 84, 90
Der Tyroler Wastel, 84
Tsching, Tsching, Tsching, 90
Hans Wurst (Hannswurst), 13, 14, 19, 20, 21, 22, 23, 24, 25, 27-36, 38, 44, 45, 46, 52, 53, 54, 74, 95, 96
Harlequin, 14, 21, 22
Haupt- und Staatsaktion, 15, 16, 19, 63
Haydn, Joseph, 26, 61, 63, 81, 83, 84, 102
Lied an den Kaiser, 83
Die beliebte Symphonie, 84
Il mondo della luna, 102
Henneberg, Johann Baptist, 84, 90f
Konrad Langbart von Friedburg, 90f
Hensler, Karl Friedrich, 60, 65, 75, 77, 92, 94, 115f, 117
Kaspar der Fagottist, 94, 115f, 117

Hieber, G,. 27
Von der Poeterey, 27
Hiller, Johann Adam, 61, 62, 64-68, 78, 93, 94, 95, 99, 117
Der Dorfbarbier, 61, 62, 66, 95
Lisuart und Dariolette, 64-66, 117
Der Teufel ist los, 66
Lottchen am Hofe, 66
Die Jagd, 66
Die Liebe auf dem Lande, 66
Der Lustige Schuster, 78, 93
Hilverding von Memen, 31, 32
Hofer, Madame Josepha, 103, 121
Hof- und Nationaltheater, 35, 36, 66, 75, 79, 82, 83, 85, 111

Joseph II of Austria, 18, 34, 35, 36, 66, 72-76, 77, 78, 85

Kärntnerthortheater, 14, 15, 19, 26, 27-36, 62, 72, 74, 75, 77, 80
Kasperl, 22, 74, 75, 93
Klemm, Christian Gottlob, 31
Moralische Wochenschriften, 31
Koch, Gottfried Heinrich, 27, 28, 65
Kurz, Joseph Felix von, 20-26, 33, 63, 82
Der aufs neue begeisterte und belebte Bernardon, 23
Der neue krumme Teufel, 26, 63
La serva padrona, 33
Die Herrschaftsküche, 33
Die Weiber- und Bubenbataille, 33
Die Judenhochzeit, 33
Kurzoper, 62

Laroche, Johann von, 22, 75
Leopoldstadttheater, 43, 60, 65, 73, 74, 77, 81, 82, 93, 116, 117, 121
Lessing, Gotthold Ephraim, 19, 21, 28, 35, 108
Minna von Barnhelm, 19
Liebeskind, 107, 108, 114f, 116f
Lulu oder die Zauberflöte, 107, 108, 114f, 116f
Lopresti, Francesco de, 28
Lustigmacher, 13, 14

172

Maria Theresia, 28, 30, 31, 33
Marinelli, Karl, 43, 57, 60, 65, 73,
    74, 75, 77, 82, 93, 110, 124
    *Don Juan oder, Der steinerne
    Gast*, 57
    Aller Anfang ist schwer, 74
Martín y Soler, Vicenz, 77, 120
    Cosa rara, 77
    Baum der Diana, 77
Meyer, Sebastian, 103
Molière, Jean Baptiste Poquelin,
    38, 54, 58
Montgolfier, 72
Mörike, Eduard, 120
    Mozart auf der Reise nach Prag
Mottley, John, 65
Mozart, Leopold, 76, 80, 99
Mozart, Marie Anne Thekla, 59
Mozart, Wolfgang Amadeus, 45,
    59, 61, 66, 73, 75, 79, 80, 81,
    83, 84, 85, 93, 94, 96, 97, 99,
    100, 101, 102, 103, 104, 105-
    113, 114-130
    Bastien et Bastienne, 66
    Figaro, 73, 94
    Die Entführung aus dem Serail,
    75, 83
    Don Giovanni (Don Juan), 83
    Così fan tutte, 83
    Der Schauspieldirektor, 83
    La Clemenza di Tito, 83
    *Eine kleine Freimaurer-Kantate
    (K.623)*, 83
    Der Stein der Weisen, 84
    Die verdeckten Sachen, 95f
    Idomeneo, 99
Müller, Wenzel, 60, 77

Napoleon Bonaparte, 91, 92
Nestroy, Johann Nepomuk, 106
Neuber, Caroline, 27, 30
Nissen, George N. von, 81, 105,
    115, 117, 121, 128
Noverre, Jean-George, 34, 72

Pacassi, Freiherr von, 31
Pamina, 98, 102, 118, 119, 121f,
    123, 124, 127, 128, 129
Papageno, 18, 47, 95, 96, 102, 103,
    110, 112, 125, 126, 127
Parnassus Boicus, 27

Pepusch, John Christopher, 65
    The Beggar's Opera, 65
Perinet, Joachim, 60, 65, 75, 77,
    79, 92, 94, 102, 106, 110, 111,
    112, 115, 116, 117
    *Mozart und Schikaneder. Ein
    theatralisches Gespräch über
    die Aufführung der Zauber-
    flöte im Stadttheater*, 60, 102
    *Ein theatralisches Gespräch
    zwischen Mozart und Schik-
    aneder über den Verkauf des
    Theaters*, 60, 102
    Kaspar der Fagottist, 115, 116,
    117
Philidor, 66
    Blaise le savetier, 66
Pickelhering, 14, 61
    Pickelhering in der Kiste, 61
Porta, Nunziato, 83
    Der Ritter Roland, 83
Prehauser, Gottfried, 19-26, 27-36,
    62, 63, 65, 66, 96

Queen of Night, 46, 114-130

Richter, Joseph, 79, 91, 93
    Eipeldauerbriefe, 79, 91, 93
Ritterdrama, 18, 19
Rousseau, Jean Jacques, 66
    Le devin du village, 66

Salieri, Antonio, 73, 77
    Der Rauchfangkehrer, 73, 77
Sarastro, 114, 117, 119, 120, 122,
    123, 126, 127, 128, 129, 130
Scandello, 102
Schack, Benedikt, 84, 95f, 97
    Der Stein der Weisen, 84, 97
    Die verdeckten Sachen, 95f
    Der wohltätige Derwisch, 97-99
Schiebeler, Daniel, 64, 65, 66, 97,
    108, 117
    Lisuart und Dariolette, 64, 65,
    66, 97, 108, 117
Schikaneder, Joseph Emanuel, 19,
    43, 57, 59, 60, 61, 62, 64, 66,
    67, 68, 69, 70, 71, 72, 75, 76,
    77-92, 93-104, 105-113, 114-
    130
    Schembera, Herr von Boskowitz,
    57, 66, 68
    Thespis, 60, 86, 87, 111

Die Lyranten oder das lustige
Elend, 66-71, 78, 93
Der Luftballon, 71, 72
Das urianische Schloss, 71, 76
Balders Tod, 72
Anton der dumme Gärtner, aus
dem Gebirge, 78, 93, 94, 96
Das abgebrannte Haus, 82
Alexander, 84, 87, 88, 89f
Pfändung und Personalarrest, 84
Untreue aus Liebe, 84
Der Löwenbrunn, 84
Die Ostindier vom Spittelberg,
84
Mina und Peru, 84
Der Stein der Weisen oder, Die
Zauberinsel, 84, 107
Der Spiegel von Arkadien, 84,
85, 91, 107, 110
Der Tyroler Wastel, 84, 85, 90,
91, 121
Die Waldmänner, 85
Babylons Pyramiden, 85, 90
Das Labyrinth oder, Der Kampf
mit den Elementen, 84, 85,
90, 107, 108
Der Königssohn aus Ithaka, 85
Der Wundermann am Rheinfall,
85, 90
Hanns Dollinger oder, Das heim-
liche Blutgericht, 86
Thespis Traum, 87, 111
Tsching, Tsching, Tsching, 90
Proteus und Arabiens Söhne, 90
Konrad Langbart von Friedburg,
90f
Die Scharfschützen in Tyrol, 91
Swetards Zaubertal, 91
Der Höllenberg oder Prüfung
und Lohn, 92
Die verdeckten Sachen, 93, 95f
Was macht der Anton im
Winter? 93, 96f
Der Frühling oder Anton ist
noch nicht tot, 93
Anton bei Hofe oder das
Namensfest, 93, 94
Der Renegat oder, Anton in der
Türkey, 93
Das Haus im Walde oder,
Antons Reise nach seinem
Geburtsort, 93

Der wohltätige Derwisch, 97-99,
107
Schiller, Johann Friedrich, 19, 108
Die Räuber, 19
Schopf, Andreas, 67
Schubart, Christian Friedrich, 102
Lied eines Vogelstellers, 102
Sedaine, Michel, 66
Blaise le savetier, 66
Selliers, Joseph Carl, 19, 62, 64
Seyfried, Ignaz Ritter von, 84, 85,
90, 109, 110, 112, 115
Untreue aus Liebe, 84
Der Löwenbrunn, 84
Die Ostindier vom Spittelberg,
84
Mina und Peru, 84
Proteus und Arabiens Söhne, 90
Seyler, Sophie, 106, 107, 109
Oberon oder, König der Elfen,
106, 107, 109
Shakespeare, William, 13
Singing Simpkin, 61
Singspiel, 26, 34, 35, 60, 61-76, 77-
92, 93-104, 114-130
Soldatenstück, 18, 19
Sonnenfels, Joseph von, 29
Briefe über die Wienerische
Schaubühne, 29
Sonnleithner, Josef, 20, 37, 43, 54,
57, 60, 90
Sporck, Graf, 31
Stegreifensemble, 20-26, 27-36, 37
Stephanie, Christian Gottlob der
Ältere, 33, 83
Stephanie Gottlieb der Jüngere, 35
Der Unterschied bey Dienst-
bewerbungen, 35
Stranitzky, Joseph Anton, 14-19,
20, 21, 22, 43, 54, 57, 62, 63,
96, 97, 106
Ollapatrida des durchgetrieben
Fuchsmundi, 16, 17, 18, 26,
27, 43, 54
Das Leben und todt Doctor
Faustus, 57
Das steinerne Gastmahl, 57
Sturm und Drang, 19
Süssmayer, Franz Xaver, 81, 83,
84, 91
Moses, 83
Der Spiegel von Arkadien, 84,
91

Tamino, 45, 98, 117, 118, 119, 120, 123-130
Terrasson, Abbé von, 108, 116f
La vie de Séthos, 108, 116f
Teutsche Arien, 22, 23, 63, 67
Teutsches Nationalsingspiel, 35, 66, 72, 77, 84
Teyber, Franz, 84, 88
Alexander, 84, 88
Pfändung und Personalarrest, 84, 88
Theater an der Wien, 60, 75, 79, 87-92, 110, 111
The Beggar's Opera, 65

Umlauf, Ignaz, 66, 73
Die Bergknappen, 66
Welche ist die beste Nation? 66, 73

Velthen, Johannes, 14
Vitichal und Dankwart, die alemannschen Brüder, 27
Voltaire (Arouet, François Marie), 28, 65
Zaïre, 28
Oedipus, 28
Ce qui plaît aux dames, 65
Vulpius, Christian August, 122, 124, 125, 126, 127, 129

Wagner, Richard, 72
Weidmann, Paul, 66, 67, 73
Die Bergknappen, 66, 73
Der Bettelstudent oder, Das Donnerwetter, 67

Weiskern, Friedrich Wilhelm, 21, 26, 28, 31, 33, 66
Weisse, Christian Felix, 61, 62, 65, 66, 67, 68, 93, 94, 95, 120, 122
Der Dorfbarbier, 61, 66, 95
Die verwandelten Weiber oder, Der Teufel ist los, 65, 66
Der lustige Schuster oder, Der zweyte Theil vom Teufel ist los, 65, 93
Lottchen am Hofe, 66, 94, 95
Die Jagd, 66
Die Liebe auf dem Lande, 66
Wieland, Christoph Martin, 68, 83, 99, 106, 107, 108, 109, 112, 113, 114, 116, 124, 130
Dschinnistan, 99, 107, 108, 112, 113, 114
Tales from *Dschinnistan*: *Die Prinzessin mit der langen Nase*, 99; *Der eiserne Armleuchter*, 99; *Das Labyrinth*, 108; *Die klugen Knaben*, 130
Oberon, 107
Winter, Peter von, 84, 111
Das Labyrinth oder der Kampf mit den Elementen, 84, 111
Wölffl, J., 92
Der Höllenberg oder Prüfung und Lohn, 92
Wranitzky, Paul, 82, 91, 106
Oberon, König der Elfen, 82, 91, 106

Zitterbarth, Bartholomäus, 87, 90